THE PHILOSOPHY OF NON-ATTACHMENT

The Philosophy of Non-Attachment

(The way to spiritual freedom in Indian thought)

M. M. AGRAWAL

MOTILAL BANARSIDASS
Delhi □ Varanasi □ Patna

MOTILAL BANARSIDASS
Indological Publishers & Booksellers
Head Office : 41-U.A., Bungalow Road, Delhi-110 007
Branches : 1. Chowk, Varanasi-1 (U.P.)
2. Ashok Rajpath, Patna-4 (Bihar)

First Edition : Delhi, 1982

ISBN: 978-81-208-2189-7

Printed in India

By Shantilal Jain, at Shri Jainendra Press,
A-45, Phase-I, Industrial Area, Naraina, New Delhi-110 028
Published by Narendra Prakash Jain, for Motilal Banarsidass,
Bungalow Road, Jawahar Nagar, Delhi-110 007

One whose reason is unattached
everywhere, who has conquered
his self and freed himself from
longing—he, through renunciation,
reaches the supreme state
beyond worldly attainments.

Gītā, ch. 18, 49

CONTENTS

I

INTRODUCTION

The ideal of non-attachment is certainly the most central concern of the Indian Philosophical psychology depicting a mode of life which is at once both, spiritual and moral in character. Ever since its first appearance in the meditation of the Upaniṣadic sages, it has recurred throughout the history of Indian philosophy, as well as, has proliferated in literature, especially in the poems of the mystic saints. It's opposite 'attachment' is conceived by the thinkers as a sort of psychic cement which holds together various elements of the empirical self by relating the individual ego to the day-to-day world of events and actions. Without this cement the empirical self will, as it were, simply wither away, and whatever, if anything, remained of the individual will return to the realm of the *transcendental*. Yet, non-attachment and its consequent self-annihilation are, according to the sages, just the things that one ought to seek out.

In the Indian metaphysical picture of the cosmos a given life of a person is seen but one among the continuing unending series of lives within a deterministic universe. Kumaril's present life is just one act which his individual consciousness performs through his earthly body, in one segment of the universe, during a given period of time. The journey of his untiring soul is infinitely long and essentially sorrowful. Birth and death, disease, old age, ignorance, hope and despair, all combine together to make human existence a painful affair. But the cause of his suffering is to be found within him, i.e., in his attachment. There is but one escape from it all—the attainment of the first and last freedom, *Nirvāṇa*, a state in which the individual realizes an infinite peace and unvarying permanence, or, to put it minimally, a release from the cycle of rebirths. The attainment of this freedom, the highest spiritual achievement of human life, is the transcendental effect of the dissolution of empirical self. Consequently, non-attachment is considered to be a necessary condition of the realization of spiritual freedom by man. Thus, it seems, the centrality of non-attachment depends upon the value and the reality of the goal of spiritual freedom. And the worth of seeking after that freedom in turn depends upon the truth of the doctrine of rebirth, and the Indian characterization of life as essentially painful. There is, however, a sense in which, even if the doctrine of rebirth falls apart, the importance of attaining spiritual freedom remains intact, provided the claim that life is essentially painful remains valid. One might even say that the urgency of attaining that freedom dawns upon one even more vividly if there is only *one* life and that is full of sorrow. But now, one may wonder, if in the present age, given man's increased understanding of Nature and control of his destiny, life must needs be sorrowful. If sorrow is to be related to material conditions such as bodily pain, loss of fortune and ordinary psychological problems, is it not that at least some individuals in some space of human history, may hope to tilt the balance between sorrow and happiness in their favour? If it were so, it would destroy the universality of the claims in question, and encourage the belief that the so-called wisdom of the ancients was little more than an expression of their pessimistic outlook towards life.

One needs to determine, then, that character of life which makes it *essentially* sorrowful. Is sorrow inherent in certain fundamental features of human existence? Does every individual experience it, or at least in his reflections apprehend it? Is there a certain kind of sorrow that is inescapable? Further, does the idea of non-attachment have any value for those who are inclined to reject the metaphysical framework within which it is presented ? Or, for that matter, what does the idea of non-attachment really amount to? The traditional exposition of the concept offers little clarity on these issues. It is one main aim of this book to seek out answers to the above questions, and through that, present the essential spiritual nexus of Indian philosophy. It may not at all be easy to answer these questions, but we must attempt to arrive at some definite conclusions along these lines if we are to concern ourselves with assessing the alleged spiritual value of the doctrine of non-attachment. We must face the materialist squarely who, referring to the believers in the existence of the immaterial soul, says to his pupil:

"You ignorant boy, such are the fooleries of these unenlightened men. They conceive that you ought to throw away the pleasures of life, because they are mixed with pain; but what prudent man will throw away unpeeled rice which encloses excellent grain because it is covered with the husk?"

It will be necessary, then, first, to elucidate the notion of non-attachment within the common framework of different metaphysical world-pictures, and then raise the question of its value and significance for human life. A sort of answer to the latter question, for those who reject a part or the whole of Indian metaphysics, will emerge in the last two sections of Ch. III, 'Freedom' and 'The Creative Consciousness', and in Ch. IV, on the relationship of non-attachment to morality.

It has often been thought that the philosophy of non-attachment shows no regard for the fact that man is essentially a social animal, and, therefore, he has some duty towards his fellow beings. This idea, *prima facie*, arises from the fact that the notion of non-attachment is tied up with the idea of the spiritual end of freedom which is primarily a personal affair. Moreover, the philosophy of non-attachment seems to be teaching that a seeker of spiritual freedom ought not to *desire* anything, even if it is a socially good end and, further, that a man of non-attachment should maintain even-mindedness towards both pleasure and pain. Again, he should neither hate the evil nor delight in the good. Such features of non-attachnent seem to signify a state of moral neutrality. While morality is concerned not only with not doing what is wrong but also, in a more positive way, with initiating and engaging in activities which are aimed at making the world a morally better place than it is. Given human nature as it is, there will always be need for constant vigilance against evil and, therefore, of positive social action.

But, it may be urged that while the classical theory of non-attachment can perhaps satisfy the requirements of a passive morality, it is difficult to see how it could encourage positive moral action in society.

However, against this view it will be argued that both non-attachment and morality, when considered from the point of view of a sane and meaningful human life, seem to require each other. This will be seen in the fact that the natural tendency of attachment is to create an area of self-centred activity for the individual. But self-centredness is normally contrasted with virtue. Non-attachment, in some degree, therefore, seems to be required for the realization of virtue. In Ch. IV it will be seen that the popular notion that the philosophy of non-attachment is a philosophy of withdrawal from the society is grossly mistaken. Far from it, the philosophy in question provides a solid foundation for significant moral action side by side with one's personal spiritual achievements. In it, the very notion of the human being as a spiritual entity seems to imply that spiritual aim could not be divorced from the moral end.

This work is not to be considered as a comment on any particular philosophy. It is rather an attempt to evolve a coherent account of non-attachment and to clarify the rather nebulously presented notion in different philosophical and religious documents. Thus, although it refers frequently to the *Gītā*, ideas from various works have been utilized, as they appear to fit in with the purpose of this work.

REFERENCES

1. *A Source Book in Indian Philosophy*, ed. Radhakrishnan and Moore, Princeton, 1967, p. 248.

II

THE METAPHYSICAL VIEW OF LIFE

The concept of non-attachment is an integral part of a whole scheme of concepts constituting the Indian view of the world. As such, in order to understand the nature and the full significance of non-attachment it will be necessary to relate it to the Indian outlook towards life, insofar as the latter has been conditioned by their philosophical picture of reality. Although there are various philosophies of reality, there is also a framework common to all of them. Fortunately, the scheme of concepts directly relevant to our purpose corresponds to this common element in their views of reality, which can be presented briefly without invoking the technicalities of the individual systems of metaphysics.

The Indian view of the world (as reflected in Hinduism, Jainism and Buddhism) is basically without God—God, that is, resembling the one in the Judao-Christian tradition. And yet many religions have sprung from it. This may appear somewhat surprising to those who have been brought up within non-Indian religious traditions. How can there be a religion without god? One is inclined to reply that it depends upon one's definition of 'religion'. But reliance on definition is nowadays philosophically in disrepute, and for good reasons. Providing definitions does not help much, for the business of *explaining* the definition still remains. Moreover what counts as a definition is itself a quarrelsome question. Yet it must be possible to say something of what is characteristic of various social and intellectual practices that constitute different religious systems, and how can a religion without God be accommodated in that family. In other words, it should be possible to say something by way of giving the necessary and sufficient condition of x being a religious system. Now, it seems to me that any mode of life that seriously deserves the title 'religious' must include some attempt to achieve an existential awareness of that reality which lies outside our ordinary empirical consciousness of the world bound by space and time. That is, a religion, among other things, must be transcendental in appeal, involving a movement from the known to the unknown. (However, in a degenerate sense there could be religion based simply upon a belief in super-beings, i.e. gods, who existed in another world within our own cosmos, who responded to our prayers and were capable of remitting material benefits to their devotees.) In many religions this transcendental reality is identical with God, who is conceived as an infinitely powerful being, the creator and the ruler of the universe, and who could be approached for personal benefits. In Indian religions, however, the transcendental reality need not necessarily contain or be identical with that God. It was therefore, clear to the Indian sages that the idea of a religion without God is quite intelligible.

However, many classical schools have introduced

the idea of a Lord, a supreme being; and some have also accepted the Lord as the creator and the regulator of the material world. But the important point to note for our discussion is that none of the schools except one (the Qualified Non-Dualist) thinks that the ultimate spiritual goal for man is to seek unity with God conceived as above. And again only one of the schools, the Dualist, regards worship of the Lord to be essential for one's spiritual perfection. By and large, then, the role of the Lord in connection with the spiritual pursuit of man is that of a helper or a teacher rather than of being its end or object. Needless to say, then, that this conception of the role of the Lord undermines the importance of the ceremonial and ritualistic aspects of religious behaviour, to the extent of making it almost redundant for the pursuit of the ultimate goal of freedom.

Now this idea of spiritual pursuit without a necessary dependence upon God is most characteristic of the Indian concern with life and truth. The spiritual philosophy in question basicallly aims at acquiring the meditative knowledge of reality. This spiritual reality is thought to be outside the scope of human mind in the sense that it cannot be *thought* out. Thus meditation and contemplation rather than discursive reasoning are recommended. As *Kena Upaniṣad*[1] puts it : "one who does not conceive it, understands it ; but one who conceives it does not. To the man who (claims to) know it, it is the 'unknown', but to one whe does not (claim to) understand it, it is the 'known'." Meditation is supposed to bring about a personal awakening, an intuitive awareness, in which the true nature of the ultimate reality is revealed to the pursuer. In the *Upaniṣad* it is supposed that knowledge has a kind of hierarchical unity, such that the knowledge of what is at the top of the hierarchy makes the knowledge of other particular facts, in some sense, redundant. Thus, it is asked : 'What is that which being known everything else becomes known'?[2] The answer to this is that the ultimate reality, conceived objectively, is Brahman. It is the unmanifest, infinite and eternal Holy Power. The power is the hidden cause, the source and also the substance of all that subsequently exists. Thus, the sages maintain, the infinite power in its manifest nature is identical with the universal self or, as is sometimes called, the Person.

However, subjectively, the knowledge of the ultimate reality turns out to be the same as the knowledge of the true nature of the individual self or soul, an eternal and therefore divine element in man. It is through self-knowledge that breaking the bonds of attachment, one transcends the limitations of ordinary human existence.

> "The inner being of all things
> The one, controller
> who renders his own form many—
> The wise who perceive him in their self—
> They, and no others, have eternal happiness."[3]

The identity of the individual self with the infinite and eternal power implies that, even though from the empirical standpoint man is seen to be implicated in Nature, in reality he is always beyond the world. Self-knowledge removes his ignorance of this truth and reveals his true identity in the unity of Being.

> "As a mirror covered with dust
> shines brightly when it has been cleansed,
> even so the embodied self
> when it has seen the true nature of the self
> becomes united, attains its end,
> and is freed from sorrow."[4]

In some mataphysical systems (as in Sāṅkhya) Nature is conceived as a separate and eternal reality, while in others (as in Non-Dualism) it is regarded as an aspect of one and the only reality—the Brahman. In the early Upaniṣads it is not clear whether Nature is distinct from spirit in an absolute sense. But on the empirical level the distinction is clear enough to make sense of the talk of the involvement of the individual soul with Nature. And ultimately, if reality is some one thing, the Being, it is clearly spiritual rather than material. However, in Nature, there exists an endless process of creation and dissolution of successive universes. Even the Nature as a whole is thought, periodically to come to a halt and revive itself again. Such a systematically deterministic Nature seems to work (evolve, withdraw and rest) according to its own internal laws, although some explain its working by invoking the idea of God's agency, and others, His power of creation.

The involvement of the individual soul in Nature seems to take the following form. First, except for his permanent potentiality to free his soul from the forces of Nature, the working out of all other potentialities in him seems to be determined by the strict laws of Nature. Next, as in Nature everything is continually changing, the individual too, insofar as he is a part of Nature, undergoes modifications, whose critical stages are marked by birth and death. But man in respect of his being a spiritual entity (a soul) survives his physical death, although he does not become free from involvement with nature. The individual's soul retaining his subtle body, a material carrier of the psychical apparatus of the intellect and the senses, at death, leaves his gross flesh-and-blood body and is subsequently reborn in human or some other form of the Nature's evolutes.

> "As a man discards worn-out clothes
> and puts on others that are new,
> the embodied being casts off bodies old
> receiving others anew."[5]

The reason for this transmigrating destiny of a soul is to be found in the existence of a universal moral law, somehow manifest in the order of Nature. According to this law an individual's soul is impelled in his next life to receive a body of a determinate kind, which places him in a situation appropriate to what he morally deserves to be or to receive for his good and bad deeds in his previous life. This is realized through the working out of *Karma*, a potency to acquire qualities and to manifest dispositions, accumulated as an effect of one's good and bad acts. It is important to note that good *Karma* is supposed to procure life-condition which is more conducive to the attainment of the spiritual end of freedom from the bondage of life. It thus shows a necessary connection between moral and spiritual action.

All accumulation of *Karma*, good and bad, however, is due to man's attachment to people, to things and even to acts and ideas. In attachment man seeks, subjectively, an identification of his self with the object of his attachment. This he tries to achieve through possession, in one form or another, of the objects in question.

Thus, attachment is the source of man's most cherished desires upon which his whole life-movement is based, including the movement from one life to another.

> "Where one's mind is attached—the inner self
> Goes thereto with action, being attached to it
> alone. Obtaining the end of his action,
> Whatever he does in this world
> He comes again from that world
> To this world of action."[6]

The man of attachment, as each man is, struggles to protect and retain the object of his attachment, resisting carefully any encroachment upon his possessions. He creates, inwardly, his own world of longings and emotions, which he suffers or enjoys alone. We will consider in detail in the next chapter, the nature of attachment; for the time being it will suffice us to note that without attachment, metaphysically speaking, man will cease to accumulate *Karma*, and will attain peace and freedom in this very life. And having exhausted his existing *Karma*, he is no more impelled to acquire fresh qualities in another birth. The principle involved in apportioning the benefits and losses in the next life is that of retributive justice. Theoretically, this involvement of the individual in the round of births and deaths is endless, unless by spiritual action, he effects the separation of the soul from the causal order of Nature.

The next important stage in this picture of reality is the equation of self-knowledge with spiritual freedom. The concept of spiritual freedom should be considered in its two aspects—a negative one and a positive one. In the positive aspect, in its extreme form, spiritual freedom is supposed to consist in a permanent state of pure consciousness which is of the nature of bliss and eternity. This pure consciousness is either individual, or, having merged with the universal consciousness, has no separate existence. In its negative aspect (common to all the Indian religions) it is given meaning by contrast with the ordinary condition of human life which is characterized as suffering and, being causally determined, a bondage to the human soul. Further, given the doctrine of rebirth, this, bondage is seen as a continuing feature of life from one death to another. Only through spiritual enlightenment, or self-knowledge, can one free oneself from this bondage. Thus, freedom, in this case, is conceived as freedom from sorrow in the present life, and from rebirth at death. Both these aspects of freedom are variously emphasized in different schools. And both these ways of looking at freedom include the following possibility. It is the possibility that a person may achieve the transcendental state of pure consciousness even before his physical death. He is then said to be free not only from further rebirths but, in a sense, inwardly, also from the conditions (pleasures and pains) of his present life. He is then said to be in a state of living-release (*jīvanmukti*).

These differences in the conception of freedom

reflect corresponding differences in the conception of the entity that is supposed to achieve freedom and retain it. But essentially, from the empirical point of view, it is the individual person i.e., the entity that is implicated in *saṃsāra* that is supposed to attain freedom. For the soul, conceived in its purity, is, in a sense, always free. As *Kaṭha Upaniṣad* puts it[7] :

> "The wise one is not born, nor does he die
> He has not come from anywhere, nor has become anyone,
> Unborn, unchanging, eternal, original,
> He is not slain in the slaying of the body".

We have noted that according to some systems it is not conceivable that the individual may retain a personal consciousness after death following the enlightenment. It is therefore not possible to say that the released *retains* freedom in any definite sense of the term. Yet, in a negative sense he may be said to be free for ever, insofar as he cannot be said to loose his freedom having once attained it.

We find, then, that this conception of man's destiny is ideally optimistic. An individual's life is not just a random, meaningless contingency. On the contrary, it is an ordered manifestation of an underlying unity of being. Ordinarily the human mind is unaware of this truth. As such he is faced with a constant challenge of the unknown. But, through a spiritual engagement with his own self, he has a hope of uncovering the secrets of being. It is a possibility which human beings have always longed to realize. Insofar as man remains, unreflectively, busy with his day-to-day mechanical life, and, thinking of his essence to consist in his bodily identity, acts in conformity with the psychological structure of the society, he is, according to this view, in a state of alienation from his own true self as well as from the cosmic reality. This self-alienation is the cause in man of a sense of unreality, emptiness and absurdity about life. And the emptiness, in turn, is the reason why man falls in the trap of attachment. As a contemporary sage, J. Krishnamurti, has explained : "Being nothing, being a desert in oneself, one hopes through another to find water. Being empty, poor, wretched, insufficient, devoid of importance, one hopes through another to be enriched. Through the love of another one hopes to forget oneself. Through the beauty of another one hopes to acquire beauty. Through the family, through the nation, through the lover, through some fantastic belief, one hopes to cover this desert with flowers. And God is the ultimate cover. So one puts hooks into all these things. In this there is pain and uncertainty, and the desert seems more arid than ever before. Of course it is neither more nor less arid; it is what it was, only one has avoided looking at it while escaping through some form of attachment with its pain, and then escaping from that pain into detachment. But one remains arid and empty as before."[8]

Life is permeated with a tragic sense of loss, due to the impermanence of the links and relationships that cannot be maintained. This idea, that what is impermanent is a source of sorrow is very often taken for granted, as in the following dialogue between the Buddhist Nāgasena and his disciples :

"What think you, monks, is the body permanent or impermanent ?
Impermanent, Lord.
But is the impermanent painful or pleasant ?
Painful, Lord.
But is it fitting to consider what is impermanent, painful, and subject to change as, 'this is mine, this am I, this is my soul' ?
No indeed, Lord."[9]

It is unwise then to fall in attachment with, and to identify oneself with, things which are impermanent. Through self-knowledge, man should seek out the truth about his existence. The need of acquiring self-knowledge is a perennial one. And, in the acquisitive and individualistic society of today, this need is perhaps even more apparent :

"Contemporary man finds himself in a paradoxical predicament. He has more political freedom, more personal freedom from the slavery of hard work, and better health and more material advantages than his predecessors. While, in general, man had never had it so good, the future of mankind has never looked so bad. For the contemporary paradox of the human predicament is that in spite of possessing all the earmarks of happiness the inner man has rarely been more miserable. The situation can be summed up by saying that contemporary man is suffering from the malady of meaninglessness."[10]

The Indian philosopher, however, considering the universal and general features of life declares that the life of attachment, as we ordinarily know it, is inherently sorrowful. He sees in the human situation what is traditionally called 'the triad of pain'. Thus, according to Iśvarakṛṣṇa[11] the three kinds of pains prevalent in life are the following. First, we have two kinds of 'intrinsic' pains, caused by the internal conditions of the individual's body and mind. In one, on the bodily side, they arise due to the malfunctioning of various bodily humours, wind, bile and phlegm. And, in the other, on the mental side, they are said to be caused by 'desire, wrath, avarice, affection, fear, envy, grief, and the non-perception of particular objects' Next there are 'extrinsic' pains which are caused by super-human agencies such as spirits and the planets etc. Now, it is observed that all these pains are at least theoretically, removable. "—Hundreds of remedies for bodily pains are laid down by eminent physicians; for mental pains also we have easy remedies in the shape of the attainment of the objects of enjoyment—such as woman, desirable food and drink, unguents, dress, ornaments and the like. Similarly, of extrinsic pains we have easy remedies—such as expert knowledge of moral and political science, residence in safe places, etc. In the same manner, of superhuman troubles we have remedies in the shape of charms, incantations and the rest."[12] However, Iśvarakṛṣṇa contends that although these means of removing pain are available, none of them provides a complete and final removal of it. His reason for holding this view is simply the empirical fact that man's body and mind are constantly exposed to the contingencies of Nature. Man, being a part of Nature, must always be causally related to it. As such there is every likelihood of his suffering some loss or damage, resulting in pain and sorrow.

I think, however, that we can make this point more strongly in the following way. As it will be apparent later, from the psychological point of view, whatever be the loss or damage to the individual, suffering on account of that requires the background of attachment. The death, for example, of someone dear to one is a cause of sorrow to him only if he is sufficiently attached to the deceased. And, as will be seen, attachment is a natural function of the experience of pleasure and the desire to avoid pain, under the ordinary conditions of human existence. It follows that man will naturally grow into all sorts of attachments depending upon the circumstances of his upbringing. At the same time the objects of his attachment being impermanent, are just as naturally denied or taken away from him. It follows from these premises that man is constantly exposed to suffering by the very nature of his existence. The only alternative is to tackle the evil of attachment itself. As the Buddhists put it : "Now this, O monks, is the noble truth of pain : birth is painful, old age is painful, sickness is painful, death is painful, sorrow, lamentation, dejection and despair are painful. Contact with unpleasant things is painful, not getting what one wishes is painful. In short the five *Khandhas*[13] of grasping are painful."[14] But we cannot possibly deal with this problem by hoping to remove the objects of attachment from our lives altogether, or by denying ourselves the likely objects of attachment. For as long as there exists the human form of life there is bound to exist some experience of pleasure (the mere thought of being alive, perhaps) or some experience of pain which will activate the whole mechanism of attachment and sorrow. We shall have more to say about how attachment is produced etc. in the next chapter. For the present our interest is to note that asceticism could not be the answer to the problem of attachment. For asceticism aims at the denial of the likely objects of attachment, and does not directly concern itself with the psychological structure of attachment. It is through meditation rather than asceticism that one conquers attachment; and meditation is self-knowledge and not discipline through self-punishment.

"Meditation is not an escape from the world; it is not an isolating self-enclosing activity, but rather the comprehension of the world and its ways. The world has little to offer apart from food, clothes and shelter, and pleasure with its great sorrows. Meditation is wandering away from this world; one has to be a total outsider. Then the world has a meaning, and the beauty of the heavens and the earth is constant. Then love is not pleasure. From this all action begins that is not the outcome of tension, contradiction, the search for self-fulfilment or the conceit of power."[15]

From an awareness of the sorrowful character of human existence there arises a spiritual anguish in man, which leads him to look for a final dissolution of sorrow. This sorrow is not just mine or yours, it is *ours*, embedded in the very nature of life as we ordinarily know it. What drove, e.g., Buddha away from the comforts and the privileges of a palace, was not just his personal frustrations but this spiritual anguish. In this second-order awareness one sees that a life which is given up to desires, which unreflectively accepts their satisfaction as the only meaning of life, is nothing but a mechanical life of stimuli and response, in which the sense of being a free agent, of having the will to initiate, undertake and plan one's activities, is nothing but an illusion. In such a life, the motive of self, surreptitiously present in every action, destroys all beauty and freedom of life. To a reflective being such a life appears to be a mere bondage. Thus even without committing oneself to the metaphysical truths about soul and rebirth, one's awareness of the true condition of human life is sufficient to inspire him to seek a spiritual release from it.

Fortunately, it is possible for man to free himself from this bondage. Through self-knowledge, rather than dogmatic worship, burning away his attachments, inwardly awake and uninvolved in the order of causes and effects, man stands above the world's sorrowful existence. Through non-attachment alone man can hope to recognize and experience the transcendental in his own life.

"The integrated self, having abandoned attachment to the rewards of work, attains to supreme peace. The unintegrated man, because of desires, attached to the fruits of actions, remains in bondage."[16]

REFERENCES

1. Pt. 11, 3.
2. *Māṇḍūkya Upaniṣad* 1, 2, 3.
3. *Kaṭha Upaniṣad* V. 12.
4. Śvetāśvatara 2, 14. cf. Parinder, *The Indestructible Soul*, p. 31.

5. *Gītā*, ch. 2, 22.
6. *Bṛhad-āraṇyaka Upaniṣad*, IV. IV. 6.
7. II. 18.
8. *The Second Penguin Krishnamurti Reader*, p. 260.
9. Saṃyutta Nikāya iii, 66, in E. J. Thomas, *The Life of Buddha*, N. Y. 1927, p. 88.
10. J. R. Royce, *the Encapsulated man*, Litton Educational Publishing, 64.
11. See, *Sāṅkhya-Kārikā*, art 1., Trans. S. S. Sastri, Madras, 1935.
12. Loc. cit.
13. The Khandhas or attachment groups are : form, feeling or sensation, perception, predisposition and consciousness.
14. Samyutta Nikāya, V. 42 D. See E. J. Thomas, *The Life of Buddha*, p. 87.
15. *The Second Penguin Krishnamurti Reader* p. 9.
16. *Gītā* Ch. 5 : 12.

III

THE NATURE OF NON-ATTACHMENT

We have seen in the previous chapter that what is common to the Indian mataphysical pictures of reality is basically a certain conception of man, his relationship with nature, and the supreme end of human life. A human being, whatever else he may be, is essentially a spiritual entity, endowed with the potential power of transcending the limitations of the world of time and space, not only intellectually but also existentially. Further, whatever else this transcendental state may consist in (bliss, omniscience, voidness etc.), it is at least a release from the round of rebirth and its consequent sorrow. Assuming, then, that release is a real goal and that it is possible for man to be totally free from sorrow, the significance of non-attachment is seen when we enquire into the necessary conditions of realizing that end. Our concern, then, is that of discovering the rational connection between the concept of non-attachment and the concept of the end in question, together with an explanation of the nature of both. For, implicit in the doctrine of non-attachment is the claim that there is a necessary connection between non-attachment and the attainment of spiritual freedom or release. But as the state of release is a post-mortem consequence of one's spiritual achievements in the present life, it is perhaps more important to explore the connection between non-attachment and the nature of the spiritual attainment of a person in his pre-release existence.

The spiritual condition of a living being predisposed to release is characterized by a total absence of sorrow. The wider claim that non-attachment leads to release, therefore, contains a lesser claim that non-attachment is a means to the dissolution of sorrow, not only through release but also in the present life. Now, I think it will be more profitable to limit ourselves to the discussion of the lesser claim for at least two reasons. One is that the idea of post-mortem spiritual freedom has many different meanings which are difficult to grasp. Moreover a discussion of release as such is outside the scope of this essay. The other reason is that our confidence in the value of non-attachment can be maintained only if it can be established that its practice leads to the dissolution of sorrow in the life that we know on this earth, and that it shows us the way to the discovery of an authentic human living. In other words, the test of the worth of non-attachment lies in its effect upon man's life under the familiar conditions of his empirical existence. And this fact provides for an exciting venture. For now, it seems that a part of the metaphysical doctrine of release can, in principle, be verified empirically. If the philosophy of non-attachment shows us the way to wipe off sorrow from human face then it has to be taken seriously by everyone. For no one, I take it, likes his life to be sorrowful. And most certainly not if one believed that there was only one life—the one which we actually have now. Thus the theory of non-attachment turns out to have a stronger, or at least an equal, appeal to the materialists, as to the believers in the mataphysics of rebirth and Nirvāṇa. For all this, however, we would not allow that the dissolution of sorrow be the sole criterion of the worth of the way of non-attachment. Non-attachment insofar as it signified a mode of living, can not be treated just as a *means* to some other end. As a conditon of life it must be regarded as an end in itself. Further, we must consider the side-effects, if any, of acquiring that frame of mind which is characteristic of non-attachment, since the dissolution of sorrow at any cost whatsoever may not be thought to be desirable. To make this point clear, we may draw an analogy between the practice of non-attachment and the practice of medicine. If the aim of a certain drug is to remove the pain from a person's body, we would not say that the cure has been effected if the drug puts him to sleep so that he can no longer feel the pain. Nor, to consider the extreme, would we say that the person has been cured if the use of the drug stops his heart beat for ever. Similarly, in case of the practice of non-attachment, we must take into account its effect on the whole being of the person from whose life sorrow has been removed. Is a sorrowless person still a *human* person? And furthermore, is the quality and the extent of his experience of life abundantly superior to that of ours; or is it radically different so as to elude any reasonable comparison ?

ATTACHMENT

The best approach to the understanding of the nature of anything is, perhaps, to explain how it comes into existence and, while it lasts, how it interacts with its environment. Now, since non-attachment basically signifies the absence of attachment, we must attempt to explain how attachment comes into being, and, as a component of the psychological structure of human mind, what role does it play in their lives.

With regard to the causation of attachment the *Gītā* declares, "When a man dwells in his mind on the objects of sense, attachment to them is produced".[1] This is clearly too limited a view of the phenomenon in question. For the objects of the senses are not the only objects of attachment. Such abstract things as knowledge, virtue and vice, action an inaction, are also amongst the objects which one can be attached to. Moreover, the process by which attachment is produced is represented here as too intellectual, involving thinking about or considering an object mentally. While this may be true in case of attachment to abstract entities, with the objects of sensation the process seems to be more direct i.e., not involving the active will. One can be attached to almost anything which comes within the fold of experience and imagination. Thus all sorts of illusions and fancies will be included among the objects in question. Nor is it the intention of *Gītā* to limit the field of attachment in this way, since it itself mentions attachment to actions, virtues etc. We can, therefore, interpret the reference to the senses to include 'mind' as well. This will be in keeping with the traditional conception of mind, which is supposed to have an organ of its own and which functions like inner sense. In the Buddhist literature this point has been made clearly, and the production of attachment has been explained as follows[2]:

"On the six organs of sense depends contact;
On contact depends sensation;
On sensation depends desire;
On desire depends attachment;
On attachment depends existence."

We also find in the above that the immediate cause of attachment is said to be desire. But it is clear that not all sensations are desired. Moreover attachment itself can be a source of desires. This ambiguity here can be removed by making a distinction between 'primitive' desires and 'non-primitive' desires. On feeling hungry, for example, one desires food—a primitive desire. But, through experience, having learnt to distinguish between food which is nourishing and tasty and food that is not, one begins to desire certain particular types of food. This will be a non-primitive or a sophisticated desire. And one may go even further; one may get so attached to the sensation of pleasure associated with a certain type of food that he may begin to desire it even if it is unhealthy and by normal standards not even tasty. Extreme examples of such desires are cases of addictions, where one goes to unworthy extents to satisfy them and feels very unhappy on failing to satisfy them. Let us call such non-primitive desires 'further' desires. Then, we are saying, that one's attachment to certain things itself becomes the cause of having certain non-primitive desires. Thus while on the one hand attachment presupposes appropriate desires, on the other, it itself is the source of further desires.

The selective principle behind the production of attachment seems to be that of pleasure. As the *Yoga* puts it : "Attachment is the sequential attraction to pleasure."[3] That is, any object of experience which is in some way pleasurable to the self tends to condition the mind in such a way as to produce a desire to secure it again on future occasions. Thus assuming that the experience of pleasure is something which normally just *happens* (as opposed to being a product of an act of willing) to us, we can say that attachment to certain kinds of objects is natural and inevitable in human life. We must observe, however, that not all desires are rooted in attachment to things already experienced. There are many things which we desire, even though we have no personal experience of them, because we have come to believe that the procurement of those things will be pleasurable, or, in one way or another, will be conducive to the furtherance of oneself. Those are the things which one longs for, which one labours for, not because one already possesses pleasant memories of them, but because the thought of securing them appears to one much pleasing and self-gratifying. It is as though we were always working with a certain image of ourselves and the inclusion of certain successes in it makes it look healthier and brighter. Since man has no natural or essential image of himself, it must be that he constructs it for himself. And then whatever he sees fitting in with it becomes an appropriate object of desire. Such desires must however be explained as rooted in a more basic tendency of the living being to *continue* its existence. Human beings can manifest this urge, it seems, only by engaging in achivement-orientated activities.

Actions, based upon desires, *assert* and underline the existence of his being—an otherwise illusive category. The kinds of actions he performs, therefore, are naturally self-protective and self-perpetuating and they carry the image of oneself a step further on the time continuum. Let us call this basic urge to continue one's existence, i.e., to remain an experiencer or a self-conscious individual entity that one supposes oneself to be, 'self-attachment'. For surely the principle involved in this is basically the same as the one invoked in case of first-order attachment, namely, the attraction to pleasure. Since all experience of pleasure depends upon existence, existence itself must be most highly desired. Perhaps, it is action directly based on self-attachment that the *Gītā* considers impure 'passions'. "But the action done with the motive of self-gratification, under strain, impelled by I-consciousness, is considered to be of the nature of 'passion'."[4]

This notion of self-attachment can now be defined as the most general and natural disposition of mind to promote the desire of the pleasant, of the self-gratifying or beneficent. Parallel to the principle of attraction to pleasure, the sages also speak of the principle of aversion to pain. Just as there is a natural tendency to feel attracted to the objects which are in some way pleasent to the self, it is also natural to feel aversion to things which are unpleasant or positively painful. "By virtue comes pleasure, by vice pain. From pleasure comes attachment; from pain, aversion."[5]

If the truth of these principles is accepted, *prima facie* it seems that Nature has installed them to secure the maximum of benefit to the individual.

Nothing, it seems, could be better than a natural reinforcement of the attraction to the pleasant and the aversion to the painful, insofar as they both aim at achieving personal gratification and well-being. Aversion to pain clearly minimizes the chances of doing those things which may prove damaging to oneself either physically or psychologically. This is clear enough in case of physical pain. The very existence of pain, according to the Theory of Evolution, is to serve as a biological mechanism to help secure the survival of its members. This could not have been so if pain was not something one naturally felt an aversion to. Similarly in case of the psychologically unpleasant, the inclination to its avoidance could be thought to serve the purpose of self-protection. Next, the natural inclination to be attracted to the pleasant also on the whole appears to be propitious. Some linguistic philosophers (as for example L. Wittgenstein)[6] have claimed that the connection between pleasure and the tendency to want it, and between pain and the tendency to avoid it, is more than contigent, i.e., a conceptual one. Whether or not it is so is a debatable point, but empirically at least the truth of the two principles in question seems to be well founded. Given, then, the complementary nature of these principles, we can maintain that just as the attraction to pleasurable things flows from the basic desire of self-continuation, the aversion to unpleasant things is due to the complementary desire of self-protection. In fact self-protection is simply an aspect of the desire to continue one's existence. Both these principles can, therefore, be seen to be dependent upon the existence of self-attachment.

To unpack the notion of attachment further, let us now reflect upon the nature of that psychological relationship in which it is manifest, namely, the relationship between the subject and the object of his attachment. What does it subjectively mean to the individual himself to feel attached to his life, wife, property etc.? What more is there to this relation, apart from the desire to derive pleasure from it? There is no doubt that attachment is a relationship of utmost *intimacy* between the attached and the object concerned. It is indeed so intimate that the object seems to have been 'interiorized' so as to appear, subjectively, to be a part of the very *being* of the attached. But what is it for an object to be a part of one's being? Clearly, the answer is that an object can be a part of one's being only if the person concerned, in his self-consciousness, sees the object to be internally connected to himself. Let us call this perception the consciousness of 'belonging' to oneself. We can explain this notion of belonging by contrasting it with "belong" in a purely technical sense. Many things which belong to one in the latter sense are due to the sanctions of custom or law, such as the things which I may inherit or produce by my labour. Then there are certain natural properties which may be said to belong to me, such as those associated with a disease or a blood-group or a race. In all these cases the reason why something belongs to me is independent of me, in the sense that it is not a product of my mind alone. But in case of 'belonging' in the other sense, the reason why something belongs to me is entirely within myself. For, this realationship is nothing else except one's own attitude towards, and beliefs about, the object which is supposed to belong to him. If one's beliefs alter and the attitude changes, the sense of ownership in question, of the object is also destroyed. But so long as attachment is there, the subject cannot even bear to think of the obect's not belonging to him, or of its belonging to someone else. This thought, subjectively, appears to him as if he was being subjected to death, or near-death, depending upon how strong the attachment in question was. The denial of the object of attachment, to say the least, minimizes the self. It threatens the cherished illusion of the substantiality of the self.

From the above characterization of attachment the following immediate effects of its occurrence can easily be inferred. First, we can see that attachment is necessarily self-enclosing. It limits the freedom of consciousness by directing one's attention towards the objects of attachment; it makes one cling to the memories of the dead past. Consequently, it also limits the freedom of action, insofar as one's thoughts and emotions are guided by it. The stronger the attachment the more one feels obsessively inclined to dwell upon its objects. In an extreme case one's consciousness could become a total prisoner of one's attachments. Needless to say that such a mind will become dull, repetitive and insensitive. Next, attachment is that which divides the world between what is *mine* and what is not mine, and then it naturally inclines one to exploit what is not mine for the sake of what is. We shall see later that this fact is of much importance for explaining the effect of attachment upon the practice of morality. The next important implication is that attachment is that relationship which enables us to think of ourselves in terms of something else. That is, attachment is that consciousness which tends to determine my innermost self-identity. There is, of course, an *objective* description of my identity, a description as it will be given by other people, or by myself, if I looked upon myself from the point of view of history, as *one of them*. But that is not the description of my inner being, of that entity which is the unique and unitary subject of all my experiences. That entity is not a part of this historical world or scientific discourse which cannot contain in it anything unique. It exists only in relation to its own world—the world which it creates by being conscious of it. But, as things are, I am not able to catch this entity in my self-consciousness. It remains constansly elusive, and all the elements of experience to which it is related as the subject, are permanently impermanent. But if I am to give my inner being a definite identity, as I want to do, I must find something enduring, something relatively permanent, in terms of which I can give content to it's formal identity. Now, it seems to me that attachment is that condition of mind through which man, as it were, *assures* himself of the permanence of certain relationships. I give myself the identity in question by thinking of myself, essentially, as that entity to which certain objects, which in reality are external to my being, necessarily *belong*. Thus a reference to the objects of my attachment is necessarily involved in the conception of my inner being. The rest I regard as only accidental relationship. The test of this truth lies in the fact, noted earlier, that emotionally I find it horribly painful to imagine that my links with the objects of my attachment may be severed. The thought of ourselves being deprived of what *belongs* to us in attachment is surrounded by the gloom and darkness of death. Further, it is this inner identity that I *like* myself to be, that I am proud of, that I try to project upon the historical world. The consciousness of the objects of attachment, however, implies a distinction, a separation between oneself and the objects in question. From this it seems to follow that attachment must involve a process by which we feign ignorance of the necessity of thinking of ourselves as distinct from the objects of attachment. And this is realized by thinking of ourselves *in terms of* the objects in question, i.e., as the entity to which the objects belong. But now we can see that the principle of attachment lands us into a double contradiction. First by identifying oneself, in self-consciousness, with certain contingent, non-self existences, it negates the fact that in personal consciousness, i.e., in consciousness from the point of view of 'me' we must necessarily experience a duality, i.e., distinction between oneself and the objects of experience. Next, by identifying the self with only certain specific objects it places other objects into a separate category, which otherwise belong to one and the same category. That is, the objects of my attachment are internally related to me; since I try to conceive of myself as just that entity to which the objects in question belong. Yet, at the same time, similar objects belonging to the same logical type are seen to be only externally related to me. For example, my attachment to my wife makes her appear as an integral part of my being, yet existentially she has the same status as any other human person. We shall soon see the full psychological significance of these implications. For the time being it will suffice us to note that the fact of attachment implies a double-edged negation. One, it negates the fact that in consciousness generally, we separate ourselves from the objects of consciousness and, two, that two like objects, whether or not I am attached to one of them, *qua* objects belong to the same category and can only be externally related to me. The experience of attachment, therefore, must breed various conflicts within us. For nothing which in itself is a denial of other facts can become a basis of order in human life. Further, we shall see that attachment leads to self-alienation, frustration and consequently, sorrow.

We may now summarize our discussion so far, and state, by contrast with the notion of attachment, what the idea of non-attachment involves. First of all attachment arises out of the desire for the pleasant and the desire for avoiding what is contrary to it. Further it is itself a source of desires. Thus non-attachment, i.e., an absence of attachment, must signify a state of desirelessness. Thus in the *Gītā*, non-attachment is equated with the 'absence of clinging to son, wife, home and the like, and a constant equal-mindedness to all desirable and undesirable happenings'.[7] Futhermore, the full concept of non-attachment must include the idea of the absence of, what we have called, self-attachment. A reference to this is made clearly in the *Dhammapada*,[8] where a true Brāhmaṇa (i.e. a sage) is described as a person, who "casting off attachment to human things, rises above attachment to heavenly things,is separated from all attachments". In such a person, it is explained, "all desire for existence is extinguished". We see here that the destruction of self-attachment is listed among the conditions of freedom from *all* attachment. Next, we have seen that attachment is a very intimate relationship in which certain objects are seen by the attached to 'belong' to him. This consciousness that objects belong to him has the following implications : 1. That attachment is necessarily self-enclosing. 2. That it divides the world in terms of mine and not mine. 3. By giving me a false sense of identity it negates the facts, (a) that consciousness involves the apprehension of duality between myself and the rest, and (b) that *all* objects of consciousness can only be externally related to me. By contrast, then, non-attachment must signify a state of freedom in which consciousness can be easily and fully directed to any object one needs to consider. And in freedom from *mineness*, it must enable us to see others for what they are. And, through the absence of the initial crippling framework of negations, it must bring us nearer to the perception of truth.

DESIRE, EMOTION AND ACTION

The single principle of attachment provides the clue to the understanding of an individual's involvement with life. The following lines from the *Gītā* reflect clearly how the enlightened ones conceived the connection between 'self', 'desire', 'emotion', and 'action'[9] :

> Bound by hundreds of ties of desire, given over to lust and anger they strive to amass hoards of

> wealth by unjust means for the gratification of their desires.
> 'This today has been gained by me : this desire I shall attain, this is mine and this wealth also shall be mine'.
> 'This foe is slain by me and others also I shall slay. I am the lord, I am the enjoyer, I am the successful, mighty and happy.'
> Bewildered by many thoughts, entangled in the meshes of delusion and addicted to gratification of desires, they fall into a foul hell.

Our attachment to particular things of pleasure and self-attachment, manifesting into innumerable desires of all kinds, lead us straight into the field of actions and emotions. That we act in order to fulfil our desires is more than an empirical truth. It is a part of the meaning of desiring something that one is inclined to, and in suitable circumstances does, act in ways in which one thinks they can be satisfied. With emotions, however, their connection to desire is not so apparent, although, empirically, it is clear enough that the frustration and satisfaction of desires generally produce one or the other appropriate emotion. There are clearly many emotions, jealousy and shame for example, which would not be felt unless a relevant desire was present.

In this context, without committing myself to its further ethical imports, the theory of emotions which seems to me to be nearest to truth is that of Sartre.[10] Sartre has claimed a very significant and purposive role for the experience of emotion. "When the paths before us become too difficult . . . we try to change the world; that is, to live it as though the relations between things and their potentialities were not governed by deterministic processes but by magic." We try to achieve it by altering our unreflective consciousness of the object of our emotion. That is, the consciousness "tries to transform itself in order to transform the object" which is desired but, under the circumstances, is unobtainable. "Emotional behaviour seeks by itself, and without modifying the structure of the object, to confer another quality upon it, a lesser existence or a lesser presence (or a greater existence, etc.). In a word, during emotion, it is the body which, directed by the consciousness, changes it's relationship with the world so that the world should change its qualities." Thus, for example, on a sudden confrontation with a frightening object my body begins to manifest fear in my heart beat, trembling of the legs and eventually in my collapse. True, this kind of behaviour is most unsuitable for my self-defence. But according to Sartre, it is still a form of purposive behaviour involving a consciousness which alters my relationship with the danger. "It is a consciousness whose aim is to negate something in the external world by means of magical behaviour, and will go so far as to annihilate itself in order to annihilate the objects also". Similarly in experiencing the emotion of joy one may colour the world in such a way that everything in it appears to him to be possible to achieve; he is filled with a sense of magical power.

Now, what this thesis amounts to is, first, that the cause of our experience of the emotions rests in our desires to escape from the objective reality, or to attempt to make it more bearable, and, next, that this is achieved by altering our own consciousness of our relationship with that reality. Thus, for Sartre, a feeling or an experience of emotion is not in essence different from action. The former is just a degenerate form of purposive, rational action. Needless to say that for Sartre it is possible to alter our emotional responses, if we alter our conception of the world and thereby alter our personal plans of action.

Having certain relevant desires, therefore, is a necessary condition for realizing a large number of acts and emotions. But, as most actions are rarely, and emotions perhaps never, mediated by conscious will or reflection, generally a relevant desire could also be a sufficient condition for realizing an action or emotion in suitable circumstances. It seems, therefore, that a very large area of human existence is founded upon desires. The kind of desires we have and encourage, and the significance we attach to them, determine the kind of life and it's quality we experience. Of course, not every desire is to be satisfied. Prudence and morality provide us with criteria for distinguishing between those that are to be promoted and those that are to be discouraged. A human being is often quite consciously controlling and directing his desires. Most actions of human beings naturally have aims and purposes. Some of these aims and purposes are definitive of a person's character and personality which provide the main themes of his life-history. These require a long protracted effort, involving a whole array of actions, without which these aims could never be achieved. A characteristically human life is therefore action-based. While desire is the inner stimulus for action, self-fulfilment is its rationale.

Now, we have seen that ideally non-attachment implies a state of total desirelessness. But if human life is action-based, and actions have their source, fundamentally in desires, then, *prima facie*, a plea for non-attachment appears to be a recommendation for inaction. And a life of inaction, even if free from personal sorrow, is by any standard, a sad waste of a life. A theory of non-attachment, therefore, must answer the following two questions. First, it must explain how, if at all, the apparent contradiction between the idea of non-attachment and the idea of action-centred life is to be removed. Next, it must also show that actions performed with non-attachment are worthwhile, i.e., that they are truly self-fulfilling or good to the agent, or they are productive of the non-personal good aimed at by the agent, or both.

A dramatized version of the first problem embedded in the theory is presented in the Gītā. In the battlefield of Kurukṣetra, grieved at the thought of gaining victory by killing his own teachers, relatives and kinsmen, Arjuna proposes to relinquish his desire for 'kingdom, enjoyments and pleasures', and decides not to fight. But, paradoxically enough, Kṛṣṇa portrayed as an incarnation of the divine, while preaching non-attachment to desires etc., urges Arjuna to fight, providing him with various reasons for choosing to act in that way. Giving his own example, Kṛṣṇa sees no contradiction in the idea of acting with complete non-attachment.

First, he rightly observes that in human life,

action, both mental and bodily, is necessary and inevitable[11] :

> For no one even for a moment can remain without action. Helplessly all are driven to action by the impulses born of nature.

Moreover, "even the maintenance of one's physical life cannot be kept if there were no action". Thus, given the necessity and inevitability of action, the proper questions to ask in this context are those that concern the nature and the mode of action, namely, 'What sorts of actions one should engage in?' and 'In what manner should one conduct them?' Kṛṣṇa's answer to both these questions are summed up in the following[12] :

> Save work done as and for sacrifice this world is in bondage to work. Therefore, O son of Kuntī (Arjuna), do the work as a sacrifice, becoming free from all attachment.

And later He says :

> Without attachment perform always the work that has to be done for man attains to the highest by doing work without attachment.

It seems, then, that action without attachment is not only possible but, spiritually, it is the only desirable mode of conduct. We must explore this concept further, for the theory of non-attachment seems to stand or fall upon the feasibility of actions which do not have their source in desires based upon attachment.

Earlier we distinguished between primitive desires such as the desire for food on feeling hungry, and further desires such as the desire to become a successful writer, arising out of attachment to certain goals associated with pleasure. Further, we defined desire as a disposition to seek the object of pleasure. A desire is, therefore, a disposition to act. But, of course, this by itself does not imply that action without such prior disposition is impossible. What we have to determine now is what exactly is being suggested with regard to desire and action when it is said that one should work without attachment.

First, working without attachment cannot signify the absence of primitive desires. The satisfaction of primitive desires, as we have seen, is normally necessary even for one's bodily existence. Even the enlightened ones such as Buddha or Kṛṣṇa needed food, shelter, rest, and presumably were occasionally ill requiring treatment. To engage in actions procuring satisfaction of the immediate needs of life is, therefore, inevitable and necessary. It would be the limit of senselessness to suggest that, e.g., a true saint should not be concerned with avoiding injury to himself, when he easily can by making an appropriate move. Indeed this suggestion presents a paradoxical situation, since the saint, if he is not a schizophrenic, will have to decide not to choose to avoid injury to himself, and thereby he will be choosing to inflict injury to himself. For a self-conscious human agent every situation is a situation in which choice, in the minimal sense, has to be exercised. For even a decision to let things go as they are is, if a person is self-conscious, an exercise of his choice. Now, if this state of affairs can also be described in terms of the agent's desire, then total desirelessness is not only impractical but logically incompatible with the state that we describe as normal human sensibility.

We now proceed to consider the second group of desires, namely the one we have called non-primitive desires. Does non-attachment imply the extinction of this group of desires? If the answer were yes, we would be left with only the satisfaction of primitive desires. However, as we have noted, most actions of human beings are aimed at the satisfaction of some or other desire of their's. Some actions, it is true, do not relate to any conscious aim, as for example, an aimless wandering in the woods, or stopping to watch a flock of birds flying past; but even they can be, and frequently are engaged in with definite aims in mind. If human life was not characterized by definite aims and purposes, it is difficult to see how man could have made that progress in his spiritual and material achievements which he has. The evolution of the two fundamental means of civilization, namely, language and technology, could not have come about without a concentrated human effort carried over from generation to generation. And it is in turn difficult to see how such effort could be made if human beings did not have appropriate non-primitive desires which determined their aims and purposes. Almost everything which is characteristically human, as opposed to animal, such as art, science, music, philosophy and intimate personal relationship, seems to depend upon the fact that human beings harbour desires and act in order to fulfil them. The whole edifice of human life seems to collapse if we remove the sophisticated, non-primitive desires from it. It is not, therefore, desirelessness as such that could safely be recommended, but at the most a certain class or type of desires. Yet, as we know, it has often been recommended by religious ascetics, and it is also supposed to be implied by the doctrine of non-attachment. However, the lives of the enlightened ones (e.g. of Buddha, and in contemporary times, of Krishnamurti) themselves do not bear it out. Insofar as they take an active interest in spreading their wisdom to others, they must have some relevant desire to do so. The sages cannot be free from all non-primitive desires. There must be something else, then, intimated in their message of freedom from desires and actions originating from them.

THE MOTIVE OF ACTION

In Chapter two of the Gītā Kṛṣṇa says[13] :

> To action alone thou has a right and never at all to its fruits; let not the fruits of action be thy motive; neither let there be in thee any attachment to inaction.

This has often been interpreted to mean that one should act without any *concern* for the results of one's action. But, without qualifications, this interpretation could be misleading, and in its obvious sense quite irresponsible. A concern for a result is always a pre-supposition of a deliberate human action. If one was not concerned with the results which a certain action in a given set of conditions is supposed to produce, there will be no question of his *deciding* to act in that manner, or in an opposite manner. The very *raison d'etre* of a deliberation, as opposed to a mere reflexive behaviour, implies, not simply an awareness, but also some concern for the results it is deemed to produce. In fact, the lack of concern for the consequences of an action seems to be clearly condemned in the *Gītā*[14] :

> The action which is undertaken through ignorance, without regard to loss and injury, and without regard to one's human capacity—That is said to be of the nature of *dullness.*

If the recommendation of disconcern for the fruits of actions is not to amount to a plea for thoughtless or meaningless action, we must clarify the actual nature and the limits of that mode of action. Now, it seems to me that the clue to the understanding of this dictum lies in the correct analysis of 'let not the fruits of actions be thy motive'. Clearly, what is being urged here is not that one should not be concerned with the results of one's actions, but that one should not make the fruits of actions one's *motive* for acting. In order to understand this point we must look for the reasons why it might be thought so. And later, we must raise two obvious questions it invites, namely, 'What should be the right motive of action ?' and 'Is it possible to act without any motive whatsoever?' : First, it is important to realize that here the term motive is being used in a manner such that a motive is always a personal, psychologically speaking, self-centred, reason for one's action. In another sense, a motive can be seen as *the* reason for acting in a particular manner, when that aspect of the act under which it is wanted is construed from *anyone's* point of view. As distinct from this the personal motive is that aspect of an act which explains the nature of a particular agent's psychological involvement with it. To take an example, someone's act of charity will be construed from anyone's point of view to be performed for the sake of helping the beneficiaries. But the agent's personal motive could be quite different—he may be doing it only in order to promote his public image as a 'kind' or 'generous' person. It is only the latter sense, which, it seems to me, has to be invoked in order to get a sensible meaning out of the *Gītā's* pronouncement in question. Thus, what is being urged is that one should not make the fruits of action one's personal motive for acting. But this is still ambiguous. For, in our example, clearly, there are two different 'fruits of action': one, the help to the beneficiary, and the other, the promotion of the agent's public image (assuming that the act does promote his image). Now, if we take the first 'fruit', then according to the pronouncement in question, it will amount to saying that the agent should not make the benefit to the recipient his personal motive in his act of charity. But this is absurd. For, no one can engage in a deliberate act of charity without wanting to benefit the recipient. If the agent performed the act knowing or believing that it was going to harm the recipient, then his act would not be an act of charity, even though it may have the surface appearance of charity. So the agent cannot eliminate the motive that his act will bear the fruit of 'help to the beneficiary'. But, in order to perform his act successfully the agent need not make the second 'fruit' his personal motive. And what the *Gītā* is prohibiting is precisely this type of motive for acting. Let us call this type of motive the 'motive of self'. What we set out to analyze, then, amounts to the recommendation that one ought not to act with the motive of self.

As it is important to grasp the nature of the motive of self, we must reflect a little more upon it. In particular, we must explain how the two motives are distinguished from each other so as to belong to different types of motives. The first thing to note is that the motive of self is not *internal* to the act itself. As in our example, we noted that the act of charity cannot be performed at all without the motive of helping the beneficiaries. But whether or not the agent succeeds in promoting his public image through it remains a further question; it remains a contingent matter. The motive of self, in this sense, is external to the success of the act in question. Next, the motive of self is always *self-seeking*. We can explain this point as follows. First deliberate human action springs from certain desires, and are aimed at producing certain definite results, howsoever vaguely they may be conceived by the agent. Thus to *act* one must have some knowledge of what one is to do and some concern for the consequences which one thinks are going to result from his action. So far so good! But there also seems to be a second order phenomenon associated with the consciousness of the fruits of one's action. It is that apart from the knowledge and the desire of the *technical* success of the action, there is also a collateral desire of a *personal* achievement through it. The success or failure in satisfying this latter desire is accompanied by the consciousness of appropriate emotions, such as of pride or shame, exaltation or grief, power or depression etc. It is as though every action was done for the sake of boosting the agent's ego, where *success* was the real aim and not that end which the action, *if* successful, objectively achieves. The action which is intended to produce a result in the objective world, rebounds back to the agent, producing in him an emotion related to the success (or failure) in terms of which the 'me' is given content as the enjoyer (or the sufferer) of the fruits of the action. In other words, there seems always an emotionally loaded thought accompanying the consciousness of the result of one's action which can be cast in the form'*I* have achieved X', '*I* have failed to achieve X'. Phenomenologically speaking, it is this sort of consciousness which normally gives a sense of personal involvement with one's actions, and determines, subjectively, one's place in the world of relationships. I shall call this product of actions the 'me-aspect' of actions.

It is now clear that the reason why one should not act with the motive of self is that the me-aspect of actions is seen as a consequence of doing them with such motives. And it is the me-aspect of actions that makes one suffer or enjoy the world, and metaphysically speaking, binds him to it. The elimination of the motive of self from the causal nexus of an action removes the consciousness of the me-aspect of that action. Consequently there is no question of feeling proud or ashamed, joyous or grieved at the success or failure of the act; from the start the action is not performed for the sake of achieving personal success. An individual's life is then free from the emotional tremors both of delight and sorrow, achieving inwardly a state of tranquility of mind. Further, as he is no longer seeking to identify himself as the doer, the enjoyer or the sufferer of his acts, he may, subjectively, enjoy a sense of freedom from the determined effects of his action within the causal order of things. In this state of being, it is supposed that, man experiences the transcendent in his life. Perhaps this is what is meant in *Kaṭha Upaniṣad* when it says[15] :

> One who is without the active will beholds Him, and becomes freed from sorrow.

And in the *Gītā*[16] :

> He who abandons all desires and acts free from longings, without any sense of mineness or egotism—he attains to peace.

It is now possible to distinguish between non-attachment and what is, in one sense, called detachment. In detachment there is no freedom from the me-aspect of actions. Detachment is a controlled exercise of mind in which a certain problem is considered, or a situation is dealt with, mechanically and efficiently in order to approach a chosen end. In this exercise whatever is not directly conducive to that end (e.g. a certain sentiment) is simply put aside by means of suppression or forcible elimination. In this regard detachment is a-moral. With detachment one could commit a murder in coldblood, just as easily as one could sacrifice his whole life for fulfilling a social mission. But non-attachment is not a mere attitude of mind which could be cultivated by practice or which could be adopted at will. It is rather a certain disposition of consciousness, produced by actual inexistence of attachments in a person. It is not a positive state of mind, in the sense, that a man of non-attachment is constantly and consciously entertaining certain thoughts or experiencing certain emotions etc. It is rather a frame of mind in which a person is naturally disposed, or is in a causally relevant condition, to act in a certain manner and to apprehend the world in a certain way. Further, as will be seen in the next chapter, there is a logical connection between being in this condition of mind and adopting certain morally relevant attitudes and principles of action. Thus, this frame of mind is relevant to modes of thinking, feeling, as well as of acting, i.e., it is a condition of the total manifestation of life's spiritual quality. We can now summarize and connect our discussion of motives with the questions we raised earlier in this section. First, a state of total desirelessness is humanly impossible. We must satisfy many of our primitive and non-primitive desires in order to survive as a living being and to survive as a member of a human society. But what the theory of attachment requires is the removal of those desires which we have termed 'further' desires. These desires are essentially rooted in attachment, and their satisfaction requires one to act with the motive of self, which, we have seen, eventually lands one in contradictions and sorrow. The removal of such desires and the motive of self cannot be achieved through force and discipline as required by various forms of asceticism, for the practice of asceticism itself involves the motive of self. The disappearance of the motive of self, which is often hidden, is effected naturally when attachment is annihilated. The uncovering of the motives of self and the perception of one's attachment is self-knowledge. Next, there is no contradiction in a completely motiveless action. In fact very often we do engage in unintentional acts, which seem to have *causes* that cannot be identified with motives. But it does seem that deliberate human actions, which have certain specific ends to achieve, cannot be free from motives in every sense of the term. But again what the theory of non-attachment requires, essentially, is that actions should not be performed with the motive of self, and this, we have seen, does not conflict with the possibility of rational human action. Lastly, to the question 'what should be the right motive of action?', we can at present give only a negative answer, viz., that the fruit of one's action, in the sense in which we have explained, should not be one's motive in doing anything. For a positive answer to this question we must wait until the next chapter.

FREEDOM

The most important truth about non-attachment is that in it there is freedom. It is freedom from the illusory consciousness of the world, including oneself, and from the inward dependence upon the objects of attachment. We tend to conceive the world as a place for the fulfilment of our desires and ambitions. But when the world, being what it is, frustrates us, and the insatiable desire torments us, we attempt to escape from it and protect our identity by colouring the world with emotions. The terrible reality, which our desires have created, remains unchanged, and we remain constantly seeking new forms of pleasures that will satisfy. In non-attachment there is freedom from the emotional consciousness of the world. There is freedom both from the emotion of joy as well as from the emotion of grief. But what kind of freedom is this, one wonders, from which joy is absent?

In order to understand this point we must first

draw a distinction between the state of happiness and the experience of emotional joy. The former, it will be evident, is not the name of a particular kind of sensation. It is rather a state of contentment which is naturally there, when life is free from conflicts, uncertainties, distortions and stupidity. It is an aspect of that state of mind which the *Gītā* calls 'peaceful', while the emotion of joy, again to refer to Sartre, 'is characterized by a certain impatience'. "For in fact this joy has been called up by an apparition of the object of his desire. He has been told that he has gained a considerable sum of money, or that he will shortly meet someone he loves and has not seen for a long time. But although the object is 'imminent' it is not yet there, it is not yet *his*... And even when it is present, even when the friend so long desired appears upon the platform, he is still an object that delivers itself to one only little by little; the delight that we feel in seeing him again soon becomes blunted; we shall never get so far as to hold him there, in front of us, as our own absolute possession and to grasp him all at once as a whole...Joy is magical behaviour which tries, by incantation, to realize the possession of the desired object as an instantaneous totality."[17]

If we agree to the above characterization of emotional joy, we can see that having the emotion of joy, like experiencing any other emotion, is a kind of unreal action. It may better be treated as a reaction to a situation which in one way or another we cannot bear to live with. But, unfortunately, it is a futile reaction, for it attempts to achieve what is impossible to achieve, namely, the absolute possession of a desired object. The emotion can produce a temporary illusion of such achievement. But soon it has to fade away and the real will again be staring in the eyes. Moreover, it must leave behind a sense of insecurity, embedded in the sub-conscious knowledge that after all the emotion was futile. Then to deal with the constant threat of the unknown and fearful contingency, we lean on more sophisticated and protracted emotions, such as 'hope', 'ambition', 'sincerity' and 'love'. Thus, it seems that each emotion necessarily contains the germs of experiencing further emotional upsurge. The character of consciousness involved in experiencing emotions can be compared to the consciousness of dream or fantasy or hysteria. Let us imagine a person who spends most of his life sleeping, and when he wakes up he recounts many joyful dreams and none involving torment or fear. Would we say that such a life is fulfilling ? The answer is obviously 'no'. In fact such a person is not even *living* his life, for dreaming is not any kind of positive action —it's actions do not take place in the same world in which the real life is lived, even though it is a kind of survival. Nor, even the person himself, I think, would be content with the thought that he had joyful dreams, if joyful experiences were missing from his wakeful life. Dream-happiness is not a substitute for wakeful-happiness. In a similar manner, it can be maintained that the experience of life of a person who sees the world through the colouring of emotions, who is making a desperate attempt to grasp an unobtainable object, who is impatiently seeking an escape, is degenerate as compared to the quality of experience of a person whose mind is calm, whose perception is clear, who has no pressing need to play-act, and who, instead of trying to flee from the real, lives his life with total intelligence.

Emotions (and sentimentality) cripple the sensitivity and inhibit the free movement of intelligence. For sensitivity and intelligence can function only when there is freedom from conditioned beliefs and opinions and from the motive of self. But both these latter factors i.e. belief and the motive of self are involved in the emotional consciousness. First, as we have noted, having a certain sort of desire is, in appropriate circumstances, a sufficient condition of experiencing certain emotions. The class of desires in question are those which involve the me-aspect of actions. And, we have maintained, that the consciousness of the me-aspect of an action is a consequence of acting with a personal motive of self. Next, we have also said that emotional consciousness presupposes certain fundamental beliefs about human predicament. Both, these beliefs and the motive of self, are nourished by our attachments. The emotional joy, therefore, cannot be the same as true or sublime joy or happiness. For true or pure joy must be free from intensionality. It cannot be the product of a self-motivated series of cause and effect. True joy must be truly spontaneous.

In short, in non-attachment there is that freedom of consciousness in which man has inwardly pulled himself out of that situation of helplessness in which he is forced to play-act. It is freedom from the impulsive psychological forces resulting in impatience and emotional turmoil. The free human being is aware of the life-situation in a manner which does not impose upon it a false meaning and value, necessitated by a psychological need to transform the difficult and unbearable reality into a personally acceptable and manageable one. Such a subject, it is clear, apprehends and lives in truth, which must always be preferable to falsity. Further, this freedom-consciousness must in itself be a continuing source of true happiness, just as the presence of the compulsive psychological forces must always be a constant source of impatience, insecurity, irritation, and therefore unhappiness. Moreover, with work done in such a frame of mind, the agent is free from the burden of *trying* to assure himself that he is living a life that is worthwhile—that it will, in the end, produce the results he desired. And being inwardly free from the feeling of frustration in failure, the needless act of self-pity, seeking comfort in the charitable sympathy of others, will have no place in his life. Non-attachment is freedom, not of the will, but *from* the will, for it signifies the total absence of that self-centred psychological structure of desire-emotion-action which limits and distorts the perception of truth in life, resulting in unnecessary sorrow and pain.

We have seen that attachment functions as a sort of *assurance*, false as it is, that certain relations are permanent. But the need for such assurance arises from the feeling of insecurity, or of fear of non-being through impermanence. Non-attachment is freedom from fear, and through it, it is freedom from the illusion of self-identity. This illusion consists in the belief that the self is a substantial entity, one and the same throughout its changing perceptions, which has the will and the freedom to act. Without this illusion there can be no basis for fear of non-being. In freedom from fear there is true joy, that is not the product of conflict, seeking and uncertainty.

Let us now consider briefly how the psychology of non-attachment connects with the metaphysical doctrine of spiritual freedom. The sages have claimed that the work done in the spirit of 'sacrifice', i.e., without making the fruits of actions one's personal motive of action, does not lead to the accumulation of *Karma*. As we have seen in Ch. 2, *Karma*, or the merit and demerit, acquired through good and bad deeds respectively, keeps the soul implicated in the round of rebirths which it morally deserves to take. But the person who is free from the consciousness of the me-aspect of actions does not in reality earn any merit or demerit for his acts. He is, therefore, at the end of his given life of 'sacrifice', freed from the natural necessity of rebirth, attaining immortality. As Kṛṣṇa explains[18] :

> Having abandoned attachment to the fruits of actions, ever content, without being dependent, he does nothing though he is ever engaged in work.
>
> He who is content with whatever comes naturally, who has gone beyond the conflicts of pleasure and pain, who is free from jealousy, and remains calm in success and failure, he even though acting remains free from bondage.

The actions performed without attachment do not bind the agent to the order of cosmic existence, for the spiritual bondage of man consists in his own desires manifest in the motives of his actions. In motiveless action there is freedom from the shackles of life.

Now, we cannot possibly endeavour to demonstrate the truth of this metaphysical claim insofar as it is related to the twin doctrines of Karma and Rebirth. But working within the framework it is presented, we can ask if it is logically coherent. And the answer seems to be that it is. For, clearly, a man who is personally, or subjectively, unaffected by success or failure, who has removed the motive of self from his action, and who remains free from the influence of emotions, will, it seems, cease to acquire fresh dispositions to engage in self-centred activities. Consequently, he will have no *active* desire, as it were, to continue his existence as a self-seeking individual entity. And, given the theory of rebirth, it does not seem implausible to speculate that such a person will not be reborn. As he accumulates no *Karma*, he drops out of the order of cause and effect involving the succession of rebirths. This, we have seen, is the condition of spiritual freedom and immortality.

THE CREATIVE CONSCIOUSNESS

The most characteristic feature of the freedom-consciousness, which we have attributed to the mind of non-attachment, is that of creativity. In order to understand this point let us first consider what is involved in being creative. In speaking of a human being, as opposed to Nature or imaginatively programmed machine, as creative we seem to be thinking of two different things united in a single process. Of these one is the subjective consciousness of the creator and the other is his creation i.e., the object or the material produce of his skillful action. The creative consciousness is quite a puzzling thing, for, on the one hand, being *creative*, it cannot be conceived as causally determined, and on the other, it cannot be mere randomness either. I shall contend that insofar as one can comprehend it at all, it appears to be an expression of man's spiritual freedom.

We tend to think that creative consciousness can be attributed only to those who are capable of producing some specific object, normally recognized as an art-form, such as, a painting, a symphony, a poem etc. If you do not produce any such thing you may be deft, clever or skilful, but not creative. To be creative is, as it were, by definition, to create something. This view of creativity, on closer examination, appears to be grossly mistaken. Mainly, because it employs a concept of the creator in which he is reduced to a mere object like other material things in the universe. And his activity is looked upon only as a quasi-mechanical activity of production, except that what he produces is not a copy of something already existing. Further, the object produced is not seen as something personal i.e., something which has a certain meaning and significance for him, but something existing for outside observers. But if we look at creativity from the point of view of the agent's inner consciousness, or subjectivity, the picture looks quite different. Then it is the creator and his personal act of creating that becomes important. We are now thinking of the subjective relationship between the creator and the object of his creation. It must be a relationship in which the object of his creation has a personal meaning and significance to him. That is, our concern is the very mode of awareness of the agent. Thus, to understand creativity we have to understand the nature of that awareness which is called creative.

Throughout the successive stages of a creative process, the elements of the creation must appear in the creator's mind, even though he may not become fully conscious of this fact. This subtle awareness of the elements of his creation must also be logically precedent to the material realization of these elements. In an actual act of creation, the awareness and the material production of the elements are so intimately linked together that one cannot significantly talk of a temporal gap between the two. But from a logical point of view, the awareness of the elements of a creative form can be separated from the act which aims at the material realization of that form. It is quite conceivable then that an artist may fail to realize satisfactorily the elements which he is subtly aware of. Consequently, the quality of his creative consciousness may be far superior than the quality of his material creation. And some of the elements of his awareness may not be realized at all. Indeed it very often is the case. Anyone who has engaged in creating something, e.g. a painting or a poem, knows well the fact that there is often a gap between what one wants to express and what is actually produced. The creator is aware that it exists and often finds it agonizing.

But now we can see that the object of creation, considered as a specific material production, turns out to be relatively unimportant for understanding the creative consciousness. For, what man creates is not just a lump of something material; it is rather an abstraction and, therefore, a perception of the creator's mind. A man, it seems, can be creative, engaged in producing *anything* (even if similar things have existed before), performing any act, as long as his perception, his awareness of the object or act, can be characterized as creative. What are then the characteristic features of this state of consciousness?

The most important attribute of the creative consciousness seems to be the apprehension of newness. But what does this apprehension of newness consist in? First, we must note that the simple answer 'It consists in the awareness of new things' will not do. For whether or not something is new depends heavily upon our way of looking at it. Further, one and the same thing has a number of different aspects, and is relatively more or less beautiful, valuable, real etc. The apprehension of the formal unity of a thing and its relative beauty or ugliness is inseparably dependent upon our being able to look at it in a relevantly novel way. To see a thing as new, in this sense, is to be aware of it in such a way that it is not immediately recognizable, and describable in terms of familiar concepts; that it cannot be fitted in the frame of past. Thus, in the experience of newness the condition of the subject's mind is just as important as the objective qualities of the thing perceived. And, in considering a person's creative consciousness, irrespective of his material creation, the experience of newness must be explicable as internal to his awareness. How then, is it possible that a person may apprehend the world so differently that his very living becomes an expression of his creative consciousness ?

In order to answer this question we have to ask why is it that there is so little experience of newness in life. Why is life filled with repetition, routine and therefore boredom ? There is obviously something holding us up from experiencing that moment to moment newness which life essentially is. The answer seems to lie in the fact that most of our life-action is nothing but conditioned response. From the very childhood we are conditioned to think, and even to feel, about life in certain definite ways. And in this way we inherit the experience of a lengthy past of a race or a culture. At the centre of this conditioning is the 'me' which loves to feed itself in every act it undertakes. It is to the essence of a conditioned mode of apprehension, that one looks at life always from the point of view of the self. For the self *is* the accumulated conditioning. That is, the world is not seen as it might be in itself, but as something which is an object for the exploits of the self; it is something essentially *for* the 'me'. Consequently, we find it almost impossible to be able to act without the motive of self. We hardly ever allow ourselves to have the world tell its own story. To act with the motive of self presupposes that one sees oneself as an agent with a plan for the future. But the plan of the future is based in the past, the known and the conditioned; it is a projection of the past in future. Or, the future is the continuation of the conditioned past, modified through imagination. In this process there is an inevitable distortion of *what is*; the 'what is', that is, that exists independently of my conception of it as a personal end. Thus, the *what is* is, in effect, recognized in terms of 'what has been' or 'what ought to be'. Obviously, in this process, the moment to moment newness of the movement of life is completely lost.

Next, as a necessary corollary to the above, all our judgments are evaluative. The present is compared with the past and assessed in terms of the future. The present, what is *given* in experience, is caught in the conceptual net of the past. Then it is scanned for what is profitable and secure to the self. We seem to have almost no freedom to be able to look at life without comparison and evaluation. In all this there is a constant effort to make life conform to the standards of the past. It is not surprising then that in the life of conditioned-response, characterized by evaluation and the motive of self, there is very little feeling of newness.

The creative awareness seems to be quite the opposite of the conditioned state of mind. In creativity, it seems, the action must be seen as an end in itself. That is, the creative mode of awareness is not deliberately adventitious. The creative agent is not undertaking to do what he does with an eye on practical utility, or the satisfaction of personal ambition etc. His creative activity consists in the realization of the act for its own sake. But this is possible only when the act is not determined by the motive of self. Creativity, then, is living in freedom from distortions through evaluation, and from the motive of self. And this, in turn, is realized only in freedom from attachment.

It is not the human will that is creative, or else it would have created enough to make himself a super-being. To be creative is to engage in skilful action consequent upon that consciousness which is free from repetition and distortion. And a talent is simply a disposition to manifest the creative consciousness in a certain manner perfected by practice. It appears then that even an untalented man can live a life that can be called creative. In fact, the artist who concentrates on one art-form may live only a few hours of his life creatively, disregarding the rest of it. Except for his talent-centred creation, the rest of his life may be ugly and insensitive. The artist who is interested in fame and money is obviously not truly interested in creativity. Generally, the creative artist is dealing skilfully only with a small fragment of his life. But to live a whole life creatively will require integrated skilful action. And this, we have seen, is possible only when living is free from the motive of self. The test that a life is being lived creatively lies in the fact that it is free from sorrow and the agony of conflicts within the individual. Again, only in non-attachment this condition is realized. In sum, creativity is an attribute of spiritual freedom. It is an experience of the inexhaustible newness of life. If, by the motive of self, one's freedom is not restricted to a small area of action, one can be an artist of the whole life.

"Art is the absence of the 'me'. But when you neglect the whole field of life and concentrate only in a little part—however much the 'me' may then be absent, you are still living unskilfully and therefore you are not an artist of life. The absence of 'me' in living is love and beauty, which brings its own skill. This is the greatest art : living skilfully in the whole field of life."[19]

REFERENCES

1. Ch. 2, 62.
2. *Samyutta Nikāya*, xxii, 90, H. C. Warren, Buddhism in Translation, p. 156.
3. Ch. 2, 7, *Yoga-Sūtra* of Patañjali.
4. Ch. 18, 24
5. II, *Yoga-bhāṣya* of Vyāsa, trans. Rama Prasada, Sacred Books of the Hindus IV, Allahabad 1924.
6. See his *Philosophical Investigations*, Oxford.
7. Ch. 13, 9.
8. Ch. xxvi, 35, trs. S. Radhakrishnan, London 1954.
9. Ch. 16, 12, 13, 14, and 16, trs. S. Radhakrishnan.
10. Ch. *Sketch For a Theory of Emotions*, trs. P. Mairet, London 1962, pp. 63-68.
11. Ch. 3, 5.
12. Ch. 3, 9, 19, trs. S. Radhakrishnan.
13. Op. Cit., 47.
14. Ch. 18, 25.
15. *The Thirteen Principal Upaniṣads*, trs. H. E. Hume.
16. Op. Cit., Ch. 2, 71.
17. *Sketch For a Theory of Emotions*, London 1962, p. 71.
18. *Gītā*, 4, 20 and 22.
19. *The Second Penguin Krishnamurti Reader*, p. 256.

IV

NON-ATTACHMENT AND MORALITY ĀTMAN & HUMAN EQUALITY

Indian philosophy in general, and the philosophy of non-attachment in particular, has often been reproached for being amoral, and even selfish in outlook. It is thought by modern materialist thinkers that the influence of such philosophy makes a man a recluse. It's accompanying practice of meditation, renunciation and non-violence etc. puts a man outside the field of social action. When the interest in one's own personal spiritual development predominates, one is likely to accept and suffer the injustices of the traditional society. One will have no will, as it were, to try to change the prevailing social conditions, by engaging in any kind of positive moral action. The Indian representation of the world as a sad place, from where one ought to get out as soon as possible, embodies, it is thought, an extreme pessimism. It teaches a cowardly escape from the problems of existence on this earth, and pretends to be teaching how to be virtuous. Some would even go as far as to impute the social and political decay of the country, and the harbouring of evils such as the caste system in our society, to the attitude of indifference which they see as characteristic of the spiritual philosophy in question.

Now, it is not my main purpose in this Chapter to defend the so-called Indian spiritualism in general. But a few remarks would not be out of place by way of clearing the ground for our main theme here, which is a discussion of the relationship between non-attachment and morality. First, in talking about the *spiritual* philosophy of action, we must leave aside the ethico-religious injunctions of the Brāhmaṇical orthodoxy. Indian spiritualism, as we have seen, does not think it necessary to worship a personal God. As such, the various specific duties (dharmas) related to the worship of various deities etc., prescribed for individuals belonging to different strata of the society, are not the requirements of Indian spiritualism but only a narrow religious sectarianism. The spiritual outlook which we have sketched in Chapter two, reveals its universal, secular and humanistic approach to life. Take for example the most resilient institution of caste-system. According to its vulgar conception, for example, a man who can wield a sword is a better human being than a man who can make a sword, and a man who has the theoretical knowledge, e.g., of economics, is superior, as a human being, to a man who can apply it to augment wealth and material. But more wickedly, a man whose grandfather could wield a sword, although he himself cannot, and is probably a parasite on the society, is still a better man than the one who earns a honest living by making swords. In short, a person born in a higher caste, e.g., in Brāhmaṇa caste, irrespective of his ability, knowledge or character, will always be a superior person than a man born in a lower caste, e.g., in Śūdra caste, even if the latter is better than the former in every human respect. Moreover, whether a person can do or is capable of doing X or not, he still ought to do it if that is what is appropriate to his caste of birth. Now, to associate such an irrational system of beliefs with Indian spiritualism will be a clear mistake, and a great dishonour to those sages who have given to mankind a rational and experimental approach, as opposed to a faith-centred approach, to a secular search of spiritual truth, parallel to the search of scientific truth in the empirical world. Many sages have clearly spelled out the importance, for the seeker of Truth, of having respect for the moral equality of man :

> "Now, he who on all beings
> Looks as just in the Self (Ātman),
> And on the Self as in all beings
> He does not shrink away from Him."[1]

And, elsewhere it is maintained that "discerning the *ātman* in every single being, the wise man rises above the sense life and attains immortality".[2]

The message of these verses is clear enough. They, in their own way, make the point that one ought to respect a human being by regarding him, not merely as an object to be exploited for one's own purposes, but as something of an intrinsic value, or, to echo the German philosopher Kant, as 'an end in himself'. For, what can be more valuable than the divine nature itself. A human being is to be respected *as a soul*. And to respect him so is to respect him for what he is by virtue of being a soul. I think, it is clear enough that it amounts to a general injunction to take into account and attach due weight to the sentiments and the interests of other people.

It might be objected that I am reading in a lot in the idea of seeing a person as a soul. Seeing a person as a soul or *ātman*, it may be contended, is simply to regard him as an intelligent, sensitive creature. It has no necessary implication of 'respect' for persons. But this objection will be a gross misrepresentation of what is being urged in the *Upaniṣads*. For there the *ātman* is already considered as the only thing of ultimate value. The *ātman* is the only thing that exists for its own sake. And more importantly, discerning the *ātman* in every being is not just an intellectual exercise. It is to acquire an existential awareness of the unity of being. And to look on all beings 'as just in the Self' is not just a matter of adopting a nice attitude towards them, it is to *realize* the truth that in reality all beings are equals. That is, as spiritual entities, all beings have equal moral status. And then, just as one could not disrespect or mistreat oneself, a person who saw the 'self in all beings' could not possibly disregard others either. In other words, anyone who took the business of 'discerning the *ātman* in every single being' seriously would find himself committed to, and effectively engaged in, treating others as morally equal to himself. The spiritual aim then, of self-realization, if properly understood, far from alienating moral attitudes from us, necessarily implicates us in morality. A person with the discriminative knowledge of the self, inwardly unattached, naturally chooses to act from the standpoint of moral respect for persons.

The *Gītā*, perhaps, is the best conscious attempt to dispel any misgivings about the spiritual way of life in question. The spirit of a spiritual involvement with life is well summed up in the following :

"What they call renunciation, know that to be disciplined activity, O Pāndava, for no one becomes a yogī who has not renounced his selfish purpose."[3]

It is not, then escape from the demands of morality, but action in the right frame of mind and with the right motive that is recommended. We have already seen in the previous chapter, that such terms as 'non-attachment', 'desirelessness', and 'renunciation' are not to be understood in such a way as to imply inaction. Rather, they signify the personal meaning which the agent ought to attach to his actions, performed without the motive of self. Even the Buddhists and Jains, who have a strong strand of asceticism, and have described the human body in a way as to arouse a feeling of disgust for bodily existence, were widely engaged in positive moral action. The following Rock Edict of the Buddhist King Aśoka shows clearly the centrality of human concern in the practice of a Buddhist way of life :

> No living thing is to be killed or sacrificed.
> Everywhere two medical services are provided.
> These consist of the care of men and animals.
> ....
> Wells have been dug by roads,
> and trees planted to shelter men and beasts
> for welfare and happiness.
> They are busy for the welfare of prisoners

if they behave irresponsibly,
and they release those that have children,
or are ill or aged.[4]

Even the monks who retired to the caves, engaged in creative work in the fields of art and architecture, and compassionate work of treating the sick with medicine and spiritual knowledge. While the Hindus had reserved asceticism only for those who had already completed the first fifty years of life and had fulfilled their social obligations as a student, a worker and a family man.

ETHICS IN THE GĪTĀ

The argument of the previous section shows that the spiritual philosophy of non-attachment does not teach us to become a recluse, or to take no interest in matters of social morality. On the contrary its very conception of the individual person is such, that in dealing with persons, it demands a certain respect for their being, which implicates us in observing the rule of moral equality of all men. It is now time to explore what precise relationship there is between non-attachment in particular, and morality.

First, without going into the discussion of the logic of moral reasoning, we may note the following general facts about the practice of morality. To begin with, no one has so far succeeded in producing a set of moral rules which are *deduced* from human nature in general, or from human rationality in particular, and which can then be applied mechanically (syllogistically) in actual moral situations to arrive at particular moral judgments. Recently, some Existentialist thinkers[5] have gone as far as to contend that there are no such things as moral principles which can help the moral agent to make his decision. Anything which the agent *chooses* to do has moral worth provided that he chooses 'freely'. This may be going a bit too far, especially when they fail to explain what a completely and genuinely free choice would be. But, this much is clear. Moral judgments are based upon factual considerations, whose knowledge and interpretation considerably varies from individual to individual. It is therefore not surprising that different moral judgments are frequently arrived at, in one and the same situation, by different individuals. Next, we may note that if there was abundance of everything to satisfy everyone all the time, there would probably be no need for moral action, except in relation with children and other dependent creatures. But the fact is however, that the resources of human life being what they are, there will always be a need for reconciliation between the conflicting interests of free and equal individuals, which will bring in moral considerations relating to one's choices. The systems of rules which attempt to give us guidelines for bringing about moral reconciliations are notoriously many, and often not even coherent. Further, it is also important to note that in actual life, moral action is not preceded by a rational (logical) consideration of the whole case. Most of our day to day decisions have some moral implication. But we do not have time to consider all their effects. Often it is not even possible to do so for other reasons, such as lack of sufficient knowledge or understanding of the situation. In actual life, mostly we simply react to situations, with a bias of our own background conditioning, of attitudes, desires, emotions etc. Thus in actual life a mere theoretical understanding of moral values is never sufficient to produce virtuous action. Nor does it become sufficient if the will to act morally is added to it. For there is the familiar problem of what the Greeks called 'akrasia' or weakness of will.[6] When a man is overcome by desire or the sense of pleasure, or when he is unable to control his temper and acts immorally in anger etc., he seems to be acting against, as it were, his own will. Or again, when a man knowing the difference between right and wrong, resolves to do what is right in a given situation, and yet fails to act accordingly, he is said to have manifested weakness of will. (Often the weakness is not apparent to the agent, for he has cunningly covered it by false justifications of a pragmatic kind.) Moreover, if it is admitted that most people do have a rough idea of right and wrong and do wish to do what is morally right, then it becomes difficult to draw a sharp distinction between deliberate immorality and immorality due to weakness of will. I am inclined to believe that weakness of will proper is just a specially apparent case of moral weakness in general. Now, in view of the above facts about the practice of morality, it is clear that in real life what is more important is, as we shall see, that the moral agent should have the psychological freedom of a relevant kind to be able to manifest virtue spontaneously. It will be my contention that this freedom *is* the freedom from one's attachments. The realization of non-attachment creates, psychologically, the most favourable condition in which a man is naturally disposed to moral goodness.

We have seen that because of the bonds of attachment, a man conceives the world as a place for self-oriented actions. He feels and perceives the things of the world as desirable or hateful, and plans to change them in such a way as to make the world more acceptable to himself. It is always the 'me' that is at the centre of his actions in the world. He goes all the way, more and more subtly and cunningly, to realize the satisfaction of his ego, and in this process suffers from confusion and deception about other people's character etc. Consider the following case. My attachment to certain sorts of pleasure leads me to desire the company of Vasela. And my subsequent attachment to her lands me into believing that she loves me; while in fact she does not and has never said that she did or even given me the impression that she did. Now, on a later date she wishes to part company with me. This naturally hurts me and I blame her for having deceived me. My position is that she by 'loving' me made me enter into a certain relationship of commitment and mutual sacrifice, which required my making various adjustments with regard to my expectations, attitudes, ambitions etc. And now when I am relevantly changed, she wants to abandon me. I conceive it as a case of desertion by her and put the moral blame upon her. But,given the facts of the case it it clear enough that my act of blaming Vasela is nothing but an expression of my self-pity consequent upon the loss of the object of my attachment, namely Vasela. My attachment is an obstruction in the clear perception of the facts of the moral situation. Naturally then I arrive at a judgment which is morally misleading. In fact it is not a moral judgment at all. For truly, making a moral judgment requires that the moral agent is able to look and evaluate the facts of the case completely impartially. By contrast then, it is clear, that a man of non-attachment has a better chance of arriving at the right moral decision than a man of attachment. And he will also put up no resistance to the manifestation of moral goodness in the actions of other people.

To elucidate further, I would like to consider the story of the *Gītā.* If we look at the plot of the story, we find that the spiritual discourse contained in it is occasioned by an attempt to resolve a moral dilemma. As noted earlier, Arjuna, having staged the battle of Kurukṣetra, is struck by grief and lamentation at the thought of killing so many opponents who were after all relatives, teachers and friends at some or other time. He thus suggests to withdraw and forego the gain of a kingdom etc. rather than fight and win the battle. Now Kṛṣṇa first tries to put the battle in the right perspective by invoking its moral implications both for Arjuna personally and for the society at large. He then diagnoses the cause of Arjuna's apparent change of mind, and then gives him the right treatment, as it were, to bring him back to perform his *moral* duty willingly. In doing this, it seems to me, He shows the importance of the relationship between moral action, the mental state of non-attachment, and the spiritual knowledge of the true nature of human existence.

For Arjuna the battle of Kurukṣetra was simply a family quarrel over the inheritance of the family throne. He saw it as a fight against his own kinsmen, elders and teachers, in order to regain a kingdom for personal glory and pleasure. True his opponents were driven by greed and would not apportion to him his due share in the throne. But Arjuna could ignore this, make a personal sacrifice, and save the family from ruin. He would also save himself from the sin of killing his elders. Thus in all his wisdom Arjuna pleads :

> "Teachers, fathers, sons, and also grandfathers, uncles and fathers-in-law, grandsons and brothers-in-law, and other kinsmen. These I would not consent to kill even for the kingdom of the three worlds; how much less for the sake of the earth?"[7]

Moreover, he argues that in the ruin of the family its traditional laws are destroyed, which in turn, corrupts the women of the family giving rise to a confusion of castes. And such a family, Arjuna thinks, must live in hell.[8] Thus thinking within the framework of traditional virtues and vices, and personal gains and losses, Arjuna is gripped with sorrow at the thought of gaining a kingdom at such a heavy cost, namely that of the ruin of his family etc.

Now, if we examine the psychology of Arjuna's thinking, it becomes clear that both, the gain and the loss, envisaged to be involved in the battle, are in the end his own. For in the destruction of the opponents Arjuna is thinking of the corruption of his own family, and of the severance of the emotional links with his teachers and other kinsmen. In other words Arjuna is unable to think of his action independently of what we have called its 'me-aspect'. The motive of Arjuna's action in question is personal gain. And the loss is always estimated in personal terms. As the overall loss is greater than the gain, Arjuna declines to fight. Thus his decision to forego the gain of a kingdom at the cost of so many lives etc., although on the surface appears to be virtuous, but in fact is no different than sophisticated prudence coloured with the humanitarian emotions of non-violence and self-sacrifice.

How does kṛṣṇa deal with Arjuna's predicament? First in Kṛṣṇa's assessment Arjuna's decision not to fight is a case of moral weakness. But the removal of moral weakness requires a fundamental treatment. So Kṛṣṇa, characterizing the situation in moral terms, engages Arjuna in a spiritual discourse. As a result of this discourse Arjuna's conception of life is completely changed. And eventually, through self-knowledge he is able to attain that spiritual freedom with which he is naturally inclined to will and act the right thing.

Briefly, with regard to the first point, Kṛṣṇa first makes Arjuna aware of his psychological state which is that of depression and grief. He then explains that, in the situation Arjuna is in, one's actions are not to be determined either by the motive of personal gain or by the emotions of attachment to his kinsmen, but by the sense of Duty. He adds that by the circumstances of Arjuna's social status as a kṣatriya prince, it was his duty to fight the battle staged for a morally good cause. Assuming, then, that the battle was to produce morally good results, our point is that Kṛṣṇa's way of looking at the situation is completely different from the way in which Arjuna looked at it.

While Arjuna is being motivated by the thoughts of personal satisfaction, Kṛṣṇa wishes him to act from the sense of duty. In order to make Arjuna see that that is how he should be acting Kṛṣṇa helps him to attain an existential awareness of the true nature of human life. Roughly, Kṛṣṇa represents the cosmos as a predetermined order of events, in which man's spiritual freedom consists, partly, in seeing this fact for what it is, and in consequence acting in freedom from the motive of self. Then having acquired the true knowledge of reality, Arjuna is freed from the conditions of attachment. And in freedom from attachment he has no difficulty in arriving at the right decision, irrespective of how the consequences of his decision will affect him personally. That is, Arjuna is successful in putting aside the motive of self which was the only kind of motive he recognised earlier.

If the above analysis is correct, we can see that the story of Gītā underlines our contention that in actual life moral weakness can be eliminated only through non-attachment. For only in non-attachment man has that kind of freedom in which actions are not inspired and guided by the motive of self. Needless to say that such actions are the only true moral actions. Such freedom is not to be found in the life of sorrow and vexation, of rancour and spite. Only in non-attachment man attains to that purity of heart and mind when virtue becomes spontaneous action. That it is more than possible is shown by the example of Janaka, the King of Mithilā:

"It was even by work that Janaka and others attained to perfection. Thou shouldst do work also with a view to the maintenance of the world."[9]

FREEDOM AND VIRTUE

In Sections 1 and 2 I have argued that anyone who commits himself to the value of 'discerning the ātman in every single being', and of choosing to act from the position of non-attachment, naturally involves himself in acting from the moral point of view. In the present section, I wish to reverse the order of enquiry and consider if acting from moral point of view logically requires non-attachment.

To avoid any misunderstanding, I may make it clear that in thinking of the moral point of view I am not thinking of that system of values whose central concept is the ideal of self-perfection. If self-perfection could be equated with the ultimate moral end of life, it would be easy to see that morality presupposes non-attachment for we have already seen that self-realisation leading to a state of perfection, according to the philosophy in question, presupposes non-attachment. Self-perfection, however, cannot be equated with the moral end. For 'morality', among other things involves the notion of 'rights' and duties', and there can be no point in talking about one's rights and duties in relation to oneself. For instance, actions whose consequences are beneficial solely to the agent can never be *obligatory* to the agent. For if it is my duty to do X because X is good to me, it must be my moral right that X ought to be done by me. But the notion of making a moral demand from oneself for one's own sake can be given no application whatsoever. In this sense, the notion or duty to oneself is absurd.

The moral point of view which I am concerned with is essentially social in character. It is social in the sense that the very need of adopting a moral point of view arises when the interests of other people can be affected by one's action. And it is neutral in the sense that considering a case from the moral point of view amounts to considering it from *anyone's* point of view. To consider a case from anyone's point of view, in turn, is to consider completely impartially the interests of all those concerned. Thus the notion of impartiality in taking decisions to act is absolutely central to morality.

Without complicating the issue at this stage, let us consider a realistic situation in which a normal individual is placed and is required to act morally. Mallick's father is an orthodox muslim gentleman. He expects of Mallick to say his prayers everyday, and to observe such religious prescriptions as not eating pork, and keeping away from alcohol and fornication. Mallick has just returned from Europe after completing his studies. During this period, he has been converted to communism and his life style has considerably changed. He now drinks and does not mind pork. His problem is whether he should make it known to his father that he is no longer a believer, or should he lie to him pretending while in his company, that he still was a 'good' muslim. This problem arises because Mallick knows, or sincerely believes, that the revelation of his conversion would be a great shock to his father and would probably result in his father's[9] nervous breakdown. How is Mallick to act?

Well, we are not interested in answering the above question for Mallick; our concern is to discover what initial conditions must be satisfied for Mallick to be able to respond to the situation morally satisfactorily. Now it seems that the following conditions are general enough to apply to all cases of moral decision-making and actions based upon them:—

(i) Knowledge of the facts of the case;

(ii) The ability to make an assessment of the human good and harm resulting from the action based upon the decision in question;

(iii) Freedom from self-deception, i.e., the mental ability to eliminate such personal factors (motive, emotions etc.) which unconsciously influence judgment;

(iv) commitment to morality.

Of these, the first three conditions are required to be satisfied for arriving at the correct moral judgment itself, while the last one is also required to be satisfied for *acting* according to the judgment arrived at. Let us confine ourselves to the consideration of the first three conditions first. I will try to unpack them one by one and relate them to our example of Mallick's case.

The description of a human situation, in which one is required to act morally, always incorporates some evaluative concepts. This is so mainly because at the centre of this situation there is always a human being to be known or understood. In Mallick's case, for example, we have described his father as an orthodox muslim. The term 'orthodox' is clearly loaded. Yet it, or some equivalent term, is indispensable in the desired description of his religious dispositions. Again we have said that Mallick knows that on knowing about his conversion, his father would have a great shock etc. And the characterization of someone's experience as 'shock' is evaluative. Moreover, Mallick's 'knowledge' of this fact will be based upon his various beliefs about his father's character traits, beliefs and emotional dispositions etc. The process by which such beliefs are formed naturally involves *interpretation* of behaviour. But the interpretation of behaviour itself presupposes various more general beliefs which serve as principles of interpretation. Ideally, it seems, that the interpretation of behaviour presupposes the entire system of general beliefs about the nature of the human self, nature and the relationship between the two. Now the process of interpreting in question is usually an unreflective (conditioned) application of one's own beliefs. Moreover, these beliefs themselves are acquired unreflectively, and are very often coloured by our own desire to find the reality congenial.

"Man seeks to form for himself, in whatever manner is suitable for him, a simplified and lucid image of the world and so to overcome the world of experience by striving to replace it to some extent by this image. This is what the painter does, the poet, speculative philosopher, the natural scientist, each in his own way. . . . "[10] In the above quotation what Einstein says about specialized seekers of truth is in a certain way true of each of us. An ordinary man has his own day-to-day world of experience, in which, he is constantly relating himself to other people, objects and events, which are not under his control. He wishes to control the course of events, to choose freely and to satisfy his desires, but the events take their own course and his desires are often frustrated. Man fails to eliminate pain and suffering from life. The world in its totality is incomprehensible; the world in its particularity is unbearable. So man tends to distort the particular situation he is in to make it more bearable. And he invents a description of the totality so as to make it less unintelligible. Madness seems to be an extreme example of a failure to secure 'a simplified and lucid image of the world'. This image of the world gets more complicated when we are looking at it from the moral point of view. For them, as we have noted, we have to accommodate human relationships in that image. And human beings of all things are the most complicated, almost mysterious, contents of the world. Moreover, they are not of a fixed nature, in the sense, that their behaviour can be predicted or controlled in a way in which, for example, the behaviour of a material object can be predicted. To put it simply, insofar as *life* and *world* are abstractions, our understanding of moral situations must always be based upon so many suppositions and conjectures about the nature of those things that make those situations. But, unfortunately, the reasons for making the suppositions etc., as we have seen, are rooted in our desire to make the situation personally bearable to ourselves. And, in this, there is inevitable distortion. While, in the first condition listed above, our talk of "the 'knowledge' of the facts of the case" has the supposition that the foundations of this knowledge are secure and reliable. How then, in describing the facts of the case, is maximum objectivity and reliability to be assured ? What we are asking for is no less than freedom from making false suppositions, and emotional misrepresentations of the data, relevant to the case in question. I have already argued that a necessary condition of achieving this freedom is that the observer should be free from all attachment. To add, we may note that people *cling* to their beliefs (true or false), if for nothing else, at least because it fits in well with their 'simplified and lucid image of the world'.

We can now see that the satisfaction of the first condition discussed above presupposes the satisfaction of the third, namely, that of freedom from self-deception. The self-deception which we are concerned with is not of an ordinary kind. We cannot avoid this sort of deception in a way in which e.g. we can avoid being deceived by a mirage. The difference is this. In the latter case all that we need is a theoretical understanding of what a mirage is and we need not be taken in by it when we perceive it. But freedom from self-deception is a more complicated matter, for in this case the subject of deception and what one is deceived about are one and the same thing, namely, the individual's empirical self. The self is constantly changing in that new thoughts and perceptions etc. are constantly arising in one's mind. So the self that is to be free from self-deception needs to be constantly aware of its own movements. And this in practice is a very difficult state to be in. For the natural tendency of the mind is to be unaware of the fact that it is whatever it is. It is true that there is a sense in which e.g., in perceiving X, I can also be said to know that I am perceiving it. But this knowing does not necessarily imply an *actual* awareness of the fact in question. It can be explained as dispositional knowledge in the sense that if I am perceiving X, I am also in a position to become reflectively aware of the fact that it is I who is in *such and such* a state of mind. But in order that it may be possible for one to be free from self-deception one needs an actual awareness of the occurrent contents of the mind. Then by perceiving the extraordinarily cunning and subtle ways of mind, in which it interprets and reacts to the world, one may be able to distinguish between the true and the false.

Now, how shall we characterize this mode of awareness in which the hidden workings of the mind are revealed to one ? To be able to answer this question, we must reflect again upon the nature of that activity of the mind which is responsible for self-deception. Consider a case in which Mallick is deceived into thinking that someone else is bent on harming him when in fact he is not. One reason for this could be that Mallick is simply jealous of his imaginary foe. Or else, Mallick may believe that he is a humble man while in fact his practice of humility is nothing but an expression of his self-conceit. In fact, a very large area of our mental life is filled with such distortions about oneself and about others. What is the common background behind such distortions ? One obvious answer is that in such cases one's perception is not motive-free. Mallick, for example, misinterprets his foes' behaviour because he perceives it with the motive of jealousy. And similarly in other cases. In other words, the mind is constantly, at a hidden level, *choosing* to see the world and people in certain ways determined by the motives of self. Thus, the mode of awareness we are trying to characterize must be one which is free from this kind of choice-ridden perception, which is biased and distorted. Thus, in order to be free from self-deception, it is not just that we need to be aware of our thoughts and feelings etc., rather we need to be aware of these in a way in which they do not get distorted further. This second-order awareness must be a pure awareness in the sense of being motive-free.

We can now see that the awareness which reveals the hidden workings of one's mind and saves one from self-deception, is a function of non-attachment. In our explanation of the notion of non-attachment, we have noted that one characteristic feature of the unattached mind is that it does not make self the motive (in the relevant sense) of one's actions. Thus a person who actually is unattached has no unconscious motive to distort the reality of his human situation to suit his self-centredness. And insofar as the real life has a natural tendency to produce selfish motives in us, a man of non-attachment, in his pure awareness, has the natural capacity to remain uninfluenced by them. For a wholly unattached mind this must be true both at the conscious and the unconscious levels. Ideally then non-attachment implies the second-order awareness in question. Next, for similar reasons, I wish to argue that the satisfaction of the second condition, in our list also requires freedom from attachment. Consider, for example, a revolutionary who has committed himself to bringing about social change through communism. He obviously thinks that he knows what is human good and harm. But the same claim is made by the anarchist, the priest, the Liberal and so on. These claims about the knowledge of human good and harm made by different groups committed to different ideals inevitably breed contradictions, confusion and chaos in the society. We know that all of them could not be right nor could their ideals be reconciled into one homogeneous system. Basically, the reason for this difference in the knowledge of human good and harm seems to be twofold. First the knowledge of the ultimate human good and harm seems to require, as it were, the God's eye-view of the world. It seems to require answering such perennial metaphysical questions as, 'Does God exist ?', 'Is man in some sense free and immortal ?', 'Does man have a fixed destiny and purpose ?', 'Are there modes of consciousness, such that in comparison with them, the ordinary human consciousness of life in space and time, is unreal or insignificant ?' etc. This is not to say that answers to such questions *entail* propositions concerning human good and harm. It is rather that knowing the answers to such questions puts one in a position to realise what is of significance and value in life, and therefore of ultimate good or harm to man. The need for such knowledge is unavoidable in deciding about important and critical cases of morality. Take, for example, the case of a judge who knows that X, who is charged for murder, is really innocent. But the prosecution has amassed *prima facie* convincing evidence against X, which proves him guilty of murder. It seems that, in his position as an officer of the law, the judge must announce the verdict 'guilty'. But a judge, while taking legal decision, is at the same time, as a human being, also taking a moral decision. We cannot divorce the morality of the case from its legality, for no one can be a judge without being a human person. And it is clear that in order to deal with his predicament the judge will have to raise the questions of ultimate significance, truth and value. Ordinarily even the best of human mind has only a very limited understanding of life and a very dim perception of truth. This seems to be in the nature of mind itself. Thus the notions of human good and harm embodied in the ideals in question are based upon a very limited view of the nature of life, and often are simply a rationalised product of one's own conditioning. Unless we break through these limitations, how could we hope to understand what human good and harm are ?

The second reason for doubting the wisdom of the political or moral theories defining human good, is psychological. It is a fact of general individual psychology that man's action is dominated by unconscious motives. The individual's moral-consciousness is not free from personal ambitions, greed, fear and anxiety, stemming from his awareness of the contingencies and the impermanence of life, and from his lack of awareness of any spiritual significance of life which makes living a passionate meaningful concern. Moreover his behaviour is conditioned by the already existing value structure of the society. How can, then, the theorists who operate from within this framework, give us the true picture of human good and harm ?

From the above considerations it seems to follow that the cognitive sensibility of a self-seeking, competitive and ambitious individual is far from the right one to be able to satisfy the conditions of morality in question. Metaphysically speaking, only through non-attachment, as we have seen, man can acquire, as it were, the 'God's eye-view' of the world and be in the position of acting truly virtuously. However, even leaving aside the metaphysical belief in question, it is clear that only through non-attachment man can remove all the psychological hindrances to the attainment of the true knowledge of human good and harm. Finally, we must now turn to the consideration of the fourth condition namely that of moral commitment. It is obvious that a sense of commitment to morality is most important when we are thinking of involvement with larger social issues. Many of us perceive the ills or the injustices of the society, but do not go as far as engaging in appropriate moral action to remove them. And even if we do, our efforts are vitiated by our personal ambition and greed. I shall attribute this sort of inaction to their lack of commitment to morality. This lack is no less manifest in the personal area of our day-to-day life. Many of us who perceive the immoralities of their own acts, which no doubt benefit them, do not try to moderate them unless compelled to do so. While others try to justify them, often by arguing that since everybody else, or almost everybody else, is corrupt, they themselves would be constant losers unless they violated morality. There is, however, a very deep-rooted sort of moral inaction which is encouraged by the very structure of our society. Even our average man who earns his so called 'honest' living is not free from it. This sort of inaction can be explained as follows :—

First, the society itself is built upon inequalities, greed and fear, delicately balanced upon the arms of ambition and competition. The society encourages competition, rewards the ambitions, makes laws to protect our little islands, and talks of the general good which usually consists in little more than the satisfaction of the wishes of those few who happen to wield power in one form or another. There is so much open poverty, suffering and sadness around us, but most of us do literally nothing to diminish it. On the contrary, we see this as an opportunity for exploitation. The writer, the artist and the social benefactor (not to mention the politician) who, in the name of self-expression, helps to maintain the *status quo*, is doing the same thing. The patriot goes to war for the sake of the nation. But he ignores the fact that within each nation itself there is a constant war between its various factions. The truth is that the society is an idol of traditions, and, in trying to conform to those traditions, we worship it. But virtue is not a matter of conformity to traditions. It is true that society by its system of praise and blame manages to inculcate certain mental attitudes and certain ways of behaviour, which it calls virtuous. But praise and blame are backed by strong social and legal sanctions, and the individual's actions are based upon the hidden fear of punishment. Needless to say that such actions, even though have the appearance of morality, cannot be called virtuous. Virtue is freedom from fear and dependence upon the psychological security of traditions. In conformity there is inaction and lack of true commitment to morality.

Now, we must enquire into the reason for the lack of commitment in question and try to show what relationship it has with non-attachment. But before this, to avoid misunderstanding, we must qualify our conclusion in the following way. First, non-conformity is not the same as anarchy. The anarchist is a mere reactionary. His action is not a product of his freedom from the psychological background of conformity. Next, we must distinguish between moral commitment and moral fanaticism. The former, as I am using the term, signifies a disposition to act independently of traditions, and according to one's own free judgment. A moral fanatic, on the other hand, like any other kind of fanatic, is a man who acts in certain fixed ways, which he regards as a matter of principle, irrespective of what reasons there might be for or against acting in those ways. Thus, for example, he may regard 'not lying' a matter of principle, such that he declines to tell a lie even when it could save the life of an innocent man. The moral fanatic fails to appreciate a very important feature of moral judgments, namely that they are made for *reasons*, and when those reasons are not present, or there are different reasons, one ought to make different judgments.[11] Thus he fails to see that it may not always be morally wrong, e. g., to violate particular sanctions of an authority such as are embodied in the legal or religious traditions of a society.

Now, leaving aside the case of moral fanaticism, we can proceed to consider the cause of moral inaction or the lack of commitment, as we have explained it. First, it is a truth of general individual psychology that man's pre-spiritual attitude towards life is shaped fundamentally by his desire of personal security; this desire being the psychological manifestation of what in biology is known as the instinct of self-preservation. McDougall, for example, maintained that the 'will to live' (cp. Freud's libido) was manifest in most basic forms of behaviour based upon instincts.[12] Another notable modern psychologist Hull, following Darwin, maintains that all human and animal behaviour is motivated and based upon 'drives' such as hunger, thirst, need to avoid pain, need for rest, activity, sex etc., which serve to promote the survival of individual organism or of the species to which the individual belongs.[13]

Now, it seems to me that human society itself is an expression of that desire for self-protection. It is because we can allay our fear of extinction, and satisfy our basic desires only through cooperation (even the robbers need to cooperate amongst themselves) in a society that we naturally group together and gradually grow into more and more complex entities. All the same, it is fundamentally the motives of self that prompt us to engage in social action. Naturally, then, when social action demands self-sacrifice, it becomes a situation of conflict. Thus there is an inherent contradiction in the very existence of the society as we know it. On the one hand, the society comes into being only because the individual is, to put it bluntly, selfish—he is a member of the society simply because only through it he can hope to survive and flourish. Yet, on the other hand, no society can exist if its members are busy simply using it for the sake of promoting their own selves. In order to deal with this contradiction we introduce force and restraints of all forms, resulting in conformity and conventional morality which we have explained.

We can now see that the cause, both of the lack of moral commitment and of its reinforcement by the structure of society, we are looking for, lies in the very nature of the self-centred man. We cannot hope to see a real concern for other people in the hearts of those whose whole basis of relationship with others is self-interest. And this pattern is reinforced through conditioning which they undergo in the society. Thus there is a vicious circle, which only the individual, through his freedom of consciousness, can break. It is only when through non-attachment man succeeds in putting aside self-interest as the motive of all his actions, that he can be free to love and cooperate instead of being aggressive and exploitative.

More precisely, the connection between non-attachment and moral commitment is this. First, attachment implies possessiveness, which is a psychological relation between the ego and the object possessed. Next, if I am attached to a person, in my attempt to possess him I invariably limit his freedom; while my attachment is a limitation upon my own freedom as well. Thus, e.g., if I am attached to my wife, I would resist any action on her part which tends to remove her from me, or diminish my power over her in some way. This tendency of my mind can be described as dependence upon her. And dependence of any form is, inwardly, a limitation of one's freedom. Moreover any encroachment upon my possessions will invoke resistance on my part. This will give rise to intolerance and conformity. In short, the more attached a person is the more possessive he is, and the more possessive he is the more dependent and, consequently, more, conforming he is. But it is just this type of 'possessive' individual which we have described as the individual who lacks moral commitment and who creates that kind of society which demands conformity. Thus attachment seems to be the direct cause of the lack of moral commitment in question. Consequently, if attachment is removed, the individual will naturally be in a position to manifest virtue spontaneously.

We can now sum up the arguments of this section. We laid down four general conditions which, among other things, must be satisfied in order to effect moral action. Our discussion of these has revealed that in one way or another, they either presuppose or involve the state of mind, we have described, of non-attachment. We can, therefore, say that the possibility of true moral action demands the necessity of non-attachment. I would like to end this Chapter with a quotation from Krishnamurti : "If our behaviour is directed by the environment in which we live, controlled and shaped by it, then it is mechanical and heavily conditioned. And if our behaviour is the outcome of our own conditioned response, is it righteous?...So we must begin to find out how deeply we have discarded the morality of authority, imitation, conformity and obedience....Unless these questions are fundamentally answered for oneself, one cannot know what it is to be truly virtuous. As we said, with what ease you come out of this hypocrisy is of the greatest importance. If you merely disregard it, it does not indicate that you are moral : you might be merely psychopathic. If you live a life of routine and contentment that is not morality either... Only out of freedom can come virtue.[14]

REFERENCES

1. ĪSĀ UPANIṢAD 6, *The Thirteen Principal Upaniṣads*,Trans. R. E. Hume, London.
2. *KENOPANIṢAD*, Pt. II.5.
3. Ch. 6, 2. Trans. S. Radhakrishnan, N. Y., 1948.
4. First Major Rock Edict, see R. Thapar, *Aśoka and the Decline of the Mauryas*, P. 250 S.
5. See, for example, Sartre J. P., *Being and Nothingness*.
6. For a discussion of this problem in Western Philosophy, see *Weakness of Will*, ed. E. W. Mortimore, Macmillan, U. K.
7. Ch. 2, 34 and 35, the *Gītā*, trans. S. Radhakrishnan.
8. Op. Cit. Ch.1, 40-44.
9. Op. Cit. Ch. 3, 20.
10. ALBERT EINSTEIN.
    'On trying to understand scientific genius', *American Scholar*, XL (1971), 108.
11. For a brilliant modern study of the nature of moral judgment, See : *Moral Notions*, by J. KOVESI, Routledge, U. K.
12. See : *Introduction to Psychology*, W. McDougall.
13. See : *Principles of Behaviour*, C. Hull.
14. *The Second Penguin Krishnamurti Reader*, Ed. Mary Lutyens, PP. 210-211.

V

CONCLUSION

It is now time to say what general conclusions can be drawn from our elucidation of the notion of non-attachment and its relation to morality. There is no doubt that the Indian philosophers—sages were deeply interested in providing an answer to the question 'How ought people to live?', which is at once both moral and spiritual in character. For them, basically, there can be only *one* way of life whose central concern was the realization of *Truth.* But Truth, it seemed evident to them, could not stand in conflict with morality. On the contrary, moral value must be a manifestation of an *aspect* of spiritual action. Moreover, their concern was not to provide a pure, disinterested, statement of truth, but to show the way in which man could free himself from illusions.

The greatest illusion which man suffers from is the illusion of self-identity. He seeks to identify himself with the objects of attachment and thinks that he can thus escape from the sorrows of this world. He tries hard to bridge the gap between himself and the world by strengthening the bonds of attachment, forgetting that it is attachment itself that divides the world in the first place between 'mine' and 'not mine.' By spreading an emotional covering on the harsh realities of life he hides away from himself the intimations of truth in them. But man remains empty, deluded, and haunted by the fear of impermanence which threatens to snatch away from him all his precious possessions, and through it destroys his own self-identity.

On the one hand there is a constant effort to seek one's identification with the changing self—the thoughts and feelings—and on the other, to remain distinct from those thoughts and feelings, as that entity which thinks and feels them. That is, in the very moment to moment consciousness—'I am *this*', 'I am *that*'—there is also a vestigial awareness of not being *this* and *that*. And, since the 'this' and 'that' have fleeting existence, and I am unaware of a separate essence of my being, I am left with a feeling of nothingness—neither a *being* nor a *becoming*.

In his reflective awareness of the human situation one sees human life imbued with sorrow. One sees a purposeless destruction of human purposes. In power and knowledge one sees the pitiable limitations of man. One sees the absurdity of the ceaseless effort of will to acquire and possess in order to enrich oneself, but in vain. One sees a meaningless dissolution of all personal meanings in death.

We have seen that the answer to these fundamental problems of living is the way of non-attachment. The condition of mind characterized by non-attachment is a consequence of self-knowledge. For spiritual knowledge is never purely theoretical. It makes an impact upon one's way of life and transforms one's subjective consciousness. The removal of the shackles of attachment dissolves the subjective structure of one's identity. Man, then, no longer acts from the motive of self and is thus freed from its consequential sorrow. And for those who believe in the doctrine of rebirth, it is a freedom from a whole series of lives of sorrow, once and for all. In non-attachment man's ensnared consciousness is freed from all the *burden* of interpretation, evaluation and possession of objects for the sake of the 'me. We have seen that the character of this freedom can truly be described as creative consciousness. In non-attachment, therefore, the expression of life is not rendered dull and insensitive, on the contrary, it makes for the experience of an inexhaustible newness.

We have also seen, that the common belief that fulfilment consists in the satisfaction of self-centred desires and in the experiencing of emotions of joy, pride etc. is also mistaken. There is always a core of unhappiness underlying all satisfaction of desires. The urge to seek satisfaction of the desires in question is a manifestation of a deep conflict within us, while the emotion is the product of our inability to face the reality as it is. True fulfilment consists in actions performed with that peace of mind and tranquility which is a consequence of self-integration and spiritual freedom.

In sum, the philosophy of non-attachment far from being an eccentric or an escapist philosophy, aims at showing the way to the individual to a wholesome living. It shows one how to live a meaningful life, satisfying at once both the demands of morality and the demands of one's own creative and spiritual urges. Thus contrary to popular opinion, it is basically an optimistic philosophy. For it encourages men to action by teaching them that their spiritual destiny is in their own hands, even though their material destiny is often not. Moreover, it recognizes explicitly, that there is no possibility of living except by acting. We can overcome depression, remove fear, despair and other psychological hindrances to creative action, only by attaching the right significance to the determined material results of our actions. Through understanding of the nature of one's attachments, one is led to the attainment of an inward freedom from dependence upon the objects of the senses as well as from ideas and beliefs. In a life lived with this freedom creativity and virtue are naturally manifest.

BIBLIOGRAPHY

1. Agrawal, M. M. *Individuality and Reincarnation* (Delhi 1978).
2. Einstein, A. 'On trying to understand scientific genius', *American Scholar*, XL (1971).
3. Hull, C. *Principles of Behaviour* (London 1943).
4. Hume, R. E. trs. *The Thirteen Principal Upaniṣads* (London 1921).
5. Kovesi, J. *Moral Notions* (U. K. 1967).
6. Krishnamurti, J. *The Second Penguin Krishnamurti Reader*, ed. M. Lutyens (U. K. 1970).
7. McDougall, W. *Introduction to Social Psychology* (London 1942).
8. Mortimore, E. W., ed., *Weakness of Will* (U. K. 1971).
9. Parinder, J. *The Indestructible Soul* (London 1973).
10. Prasada, R. *Yoga-bhāṣya*, (Allahabad 1924).
11. Radhakrishnan, S, trs. *Bhagavad Gitā* (N. Y. 1948).
12. Radhakrishnan and Moore, ed. *A Source Book in Indian Philosophy* (Princeton 1967).
13. Royce, J. R. *The Encapsulated Man* (N. Y. 1964).
14. Sartre, J. P. *Being and Nothingness* trs. Hazel E. Barnes (London 1957).
15. Sartre, J. P. *Sketch for a Theory of Emotion* trs. P. Mairet (London 1962).
16. Sastri, S. S. trs. *Sāṅkhya Kārikā* (Madras 1935).
17. Thomas, E. J. *The Life of Buddha* (N. Y. 1927).
18. Warren, H. C. *Buddhism in Translation* (Cambridge, Mass. 1915).
19. Wittgenstein, L. *Philosophical Investigations* (Oxford 1958).

INDEX